Dogs Art

Hand Drawn

Adults Coloring Page

Cretted by Ally Nathaniel

Illustrated by Syuzan Melikyan

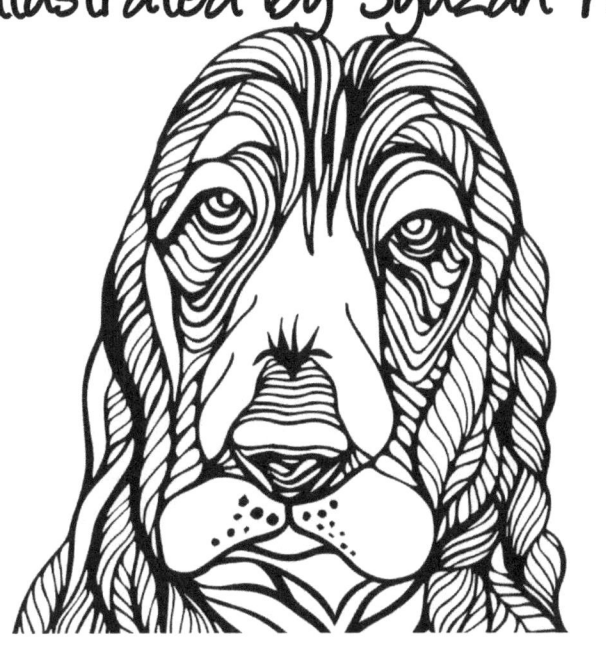

ISBN-13:978-1523838561

ISBN-10:1523838566

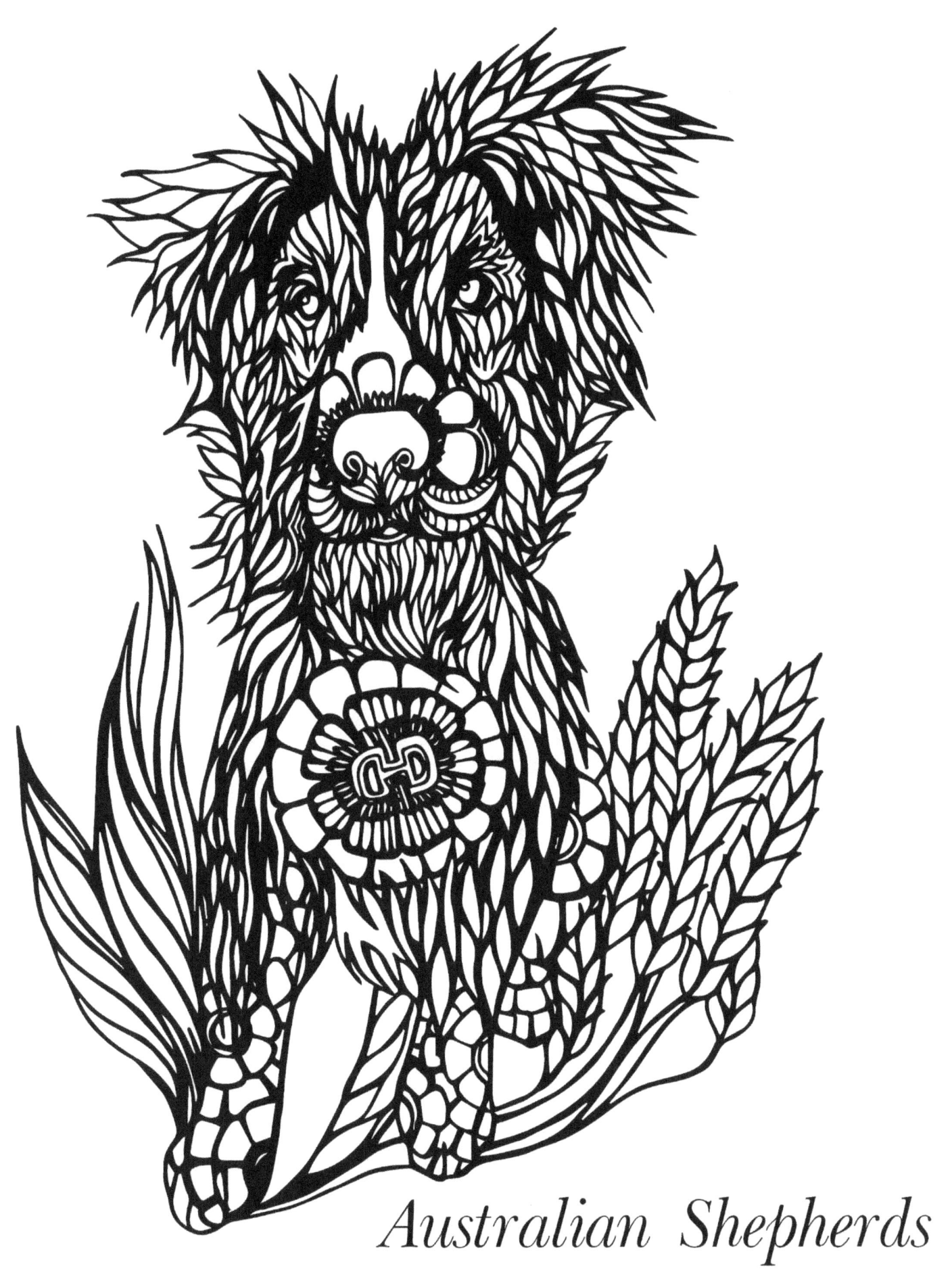

Australian Shepherds

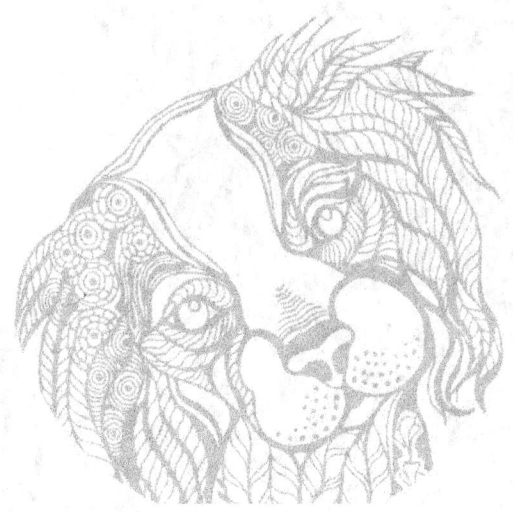

Beagle

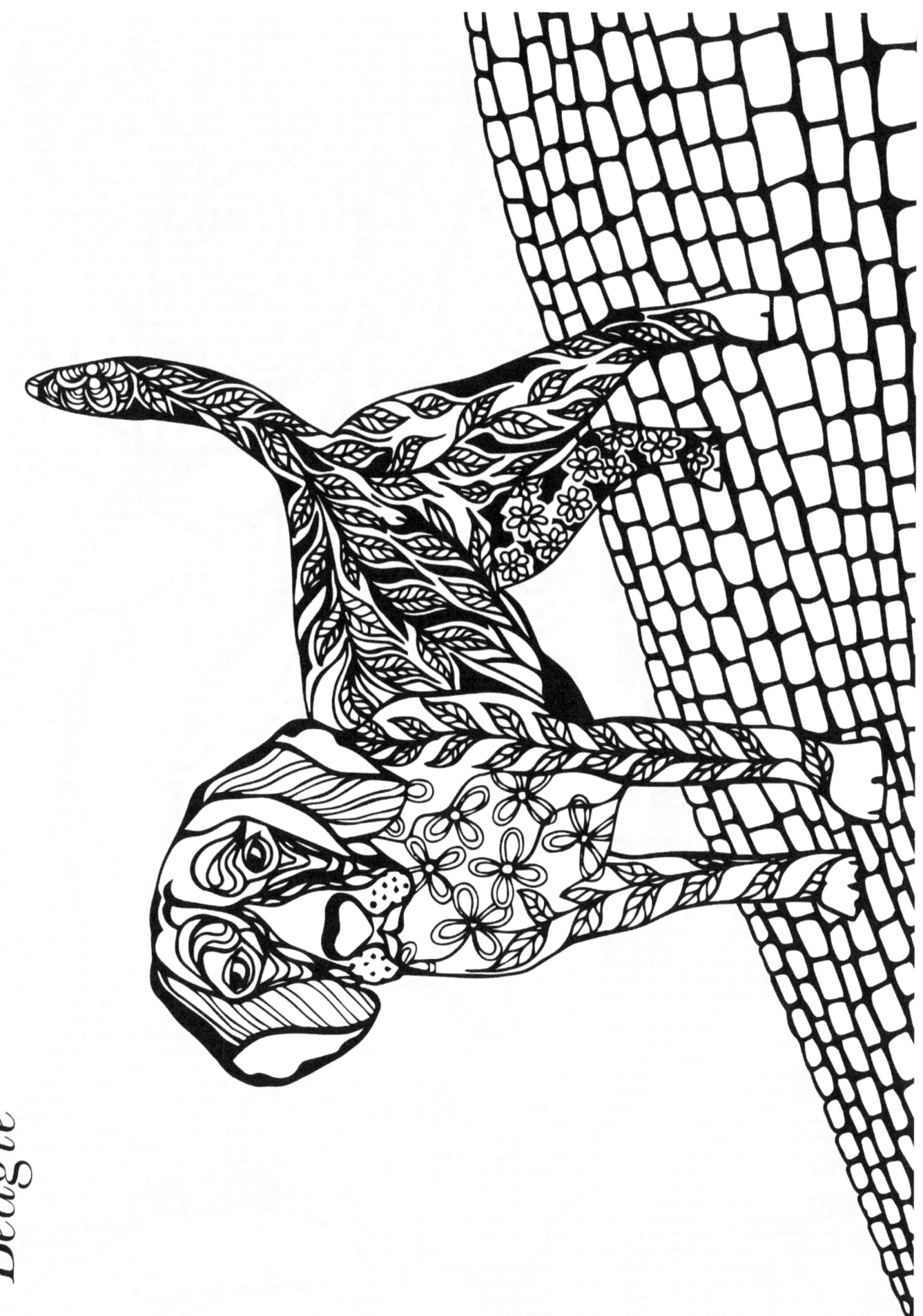

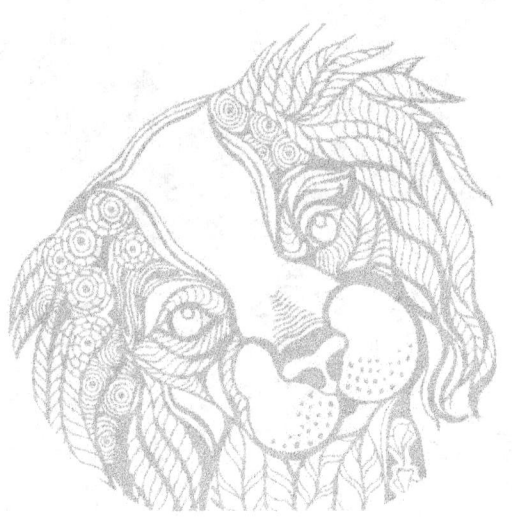

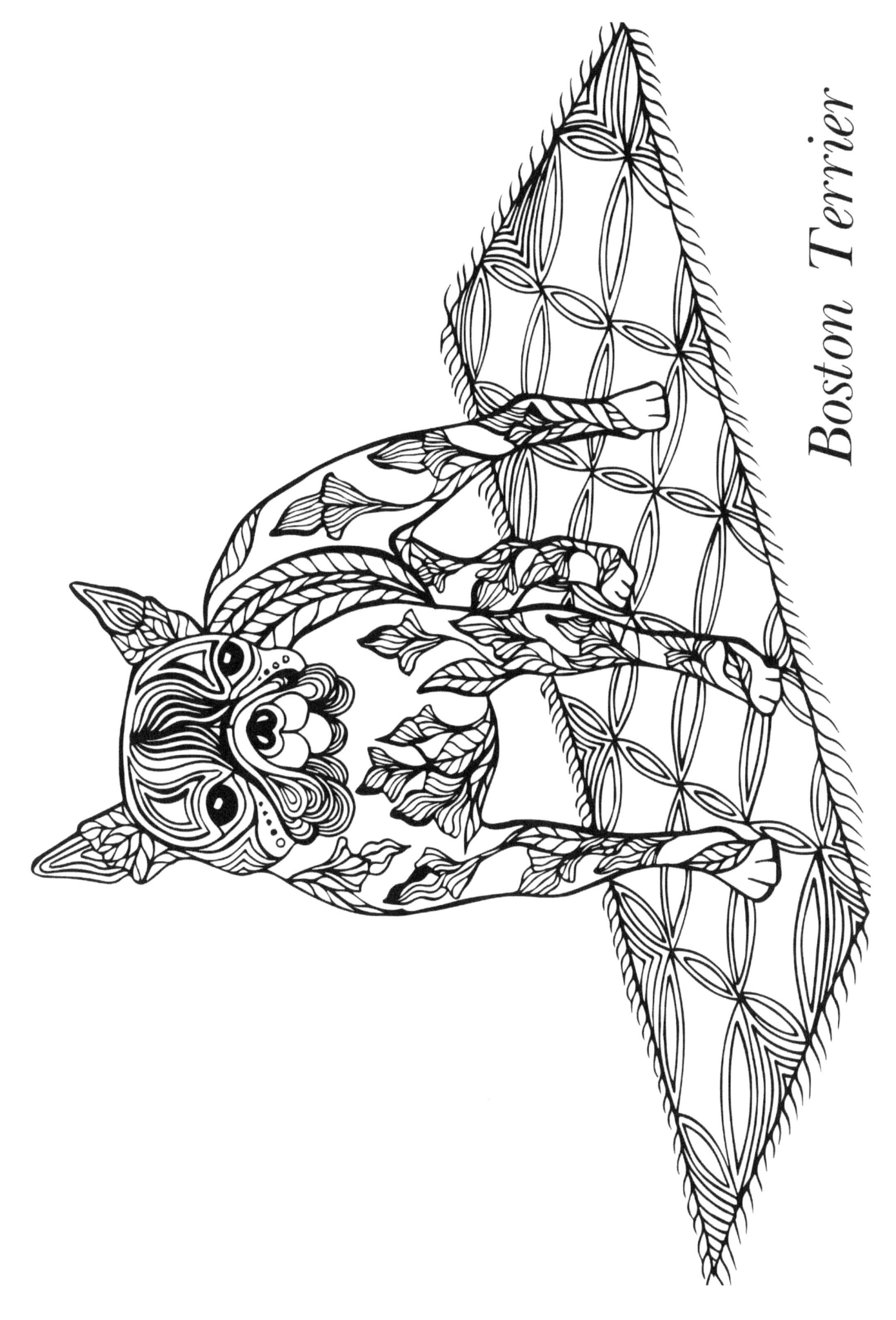

Boston Terrier

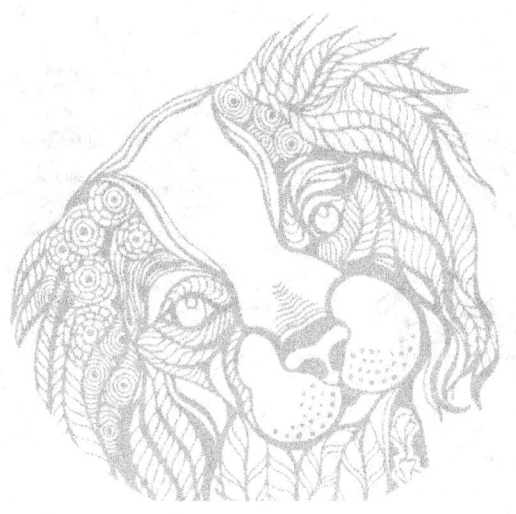

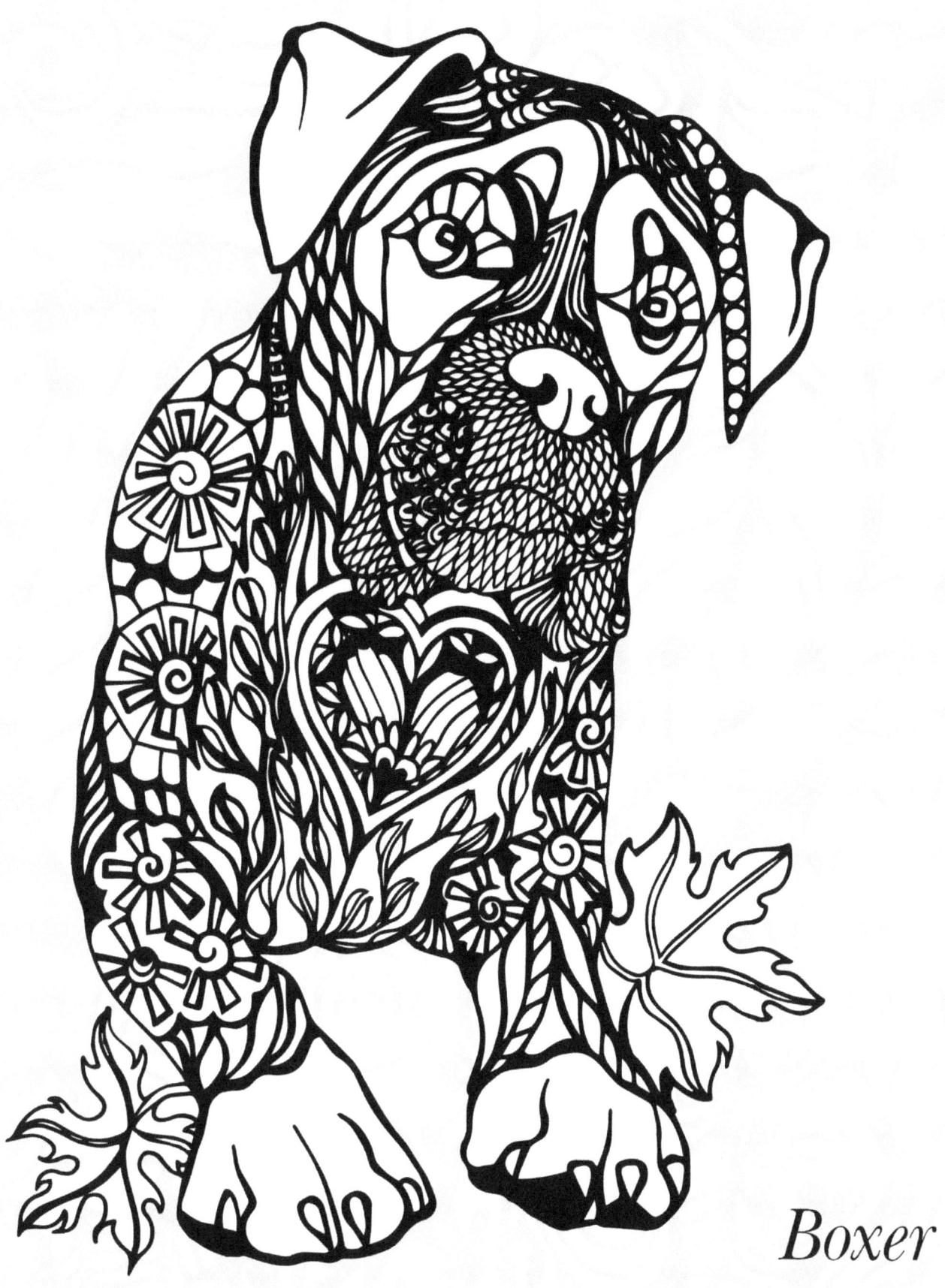

Boxer

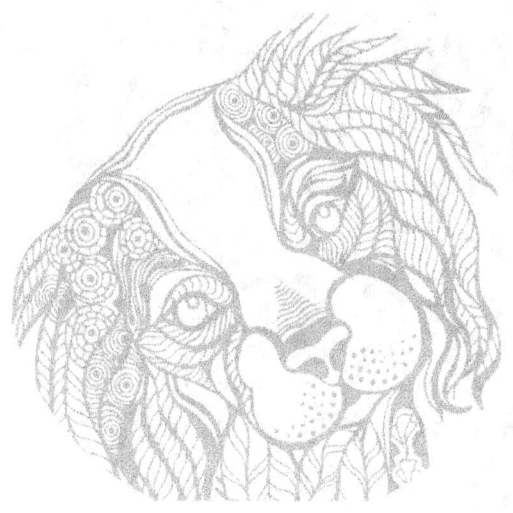

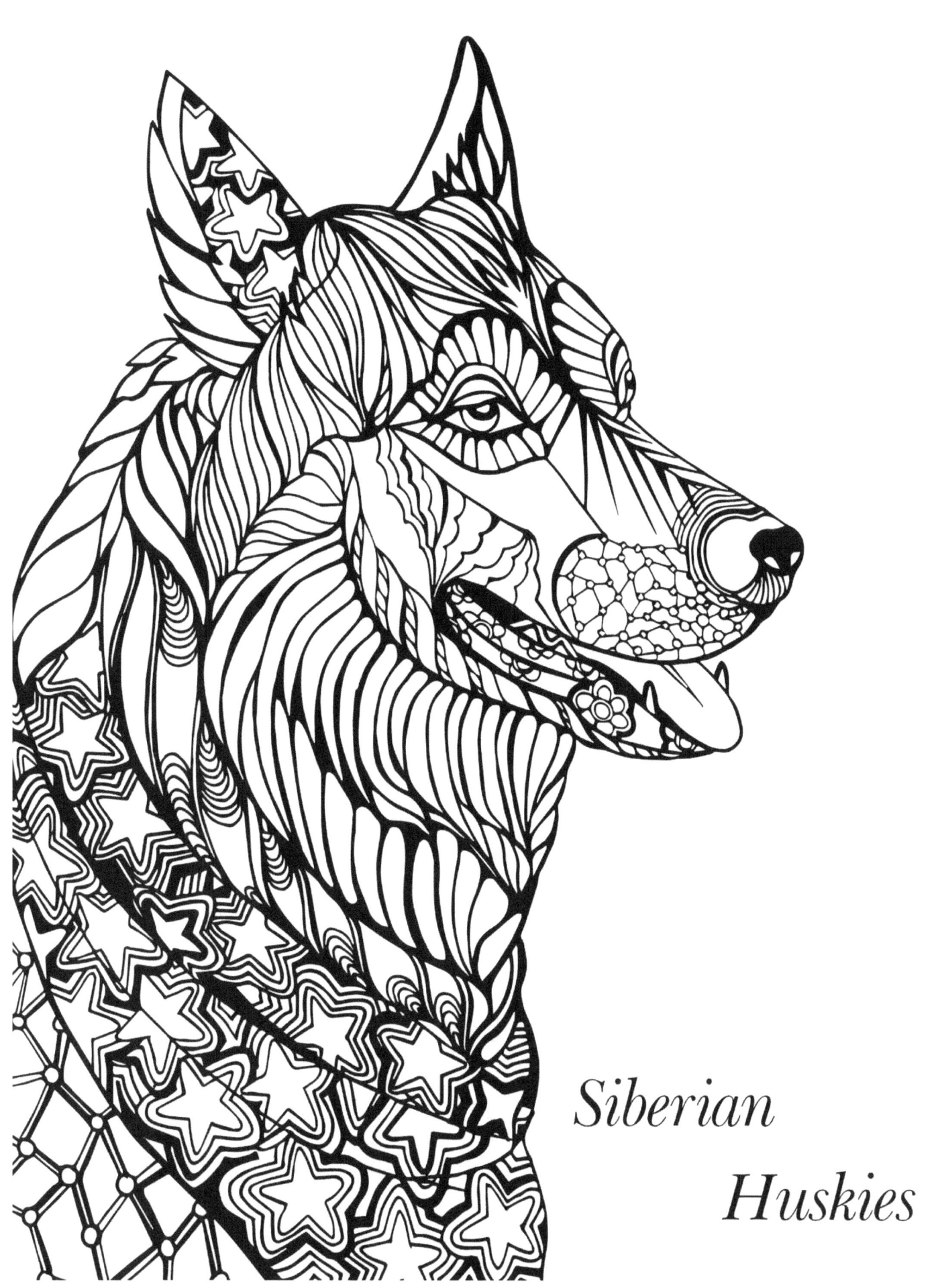

Siberian

Huskies

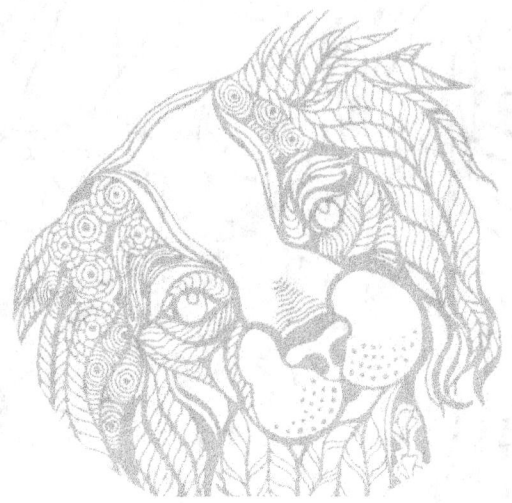

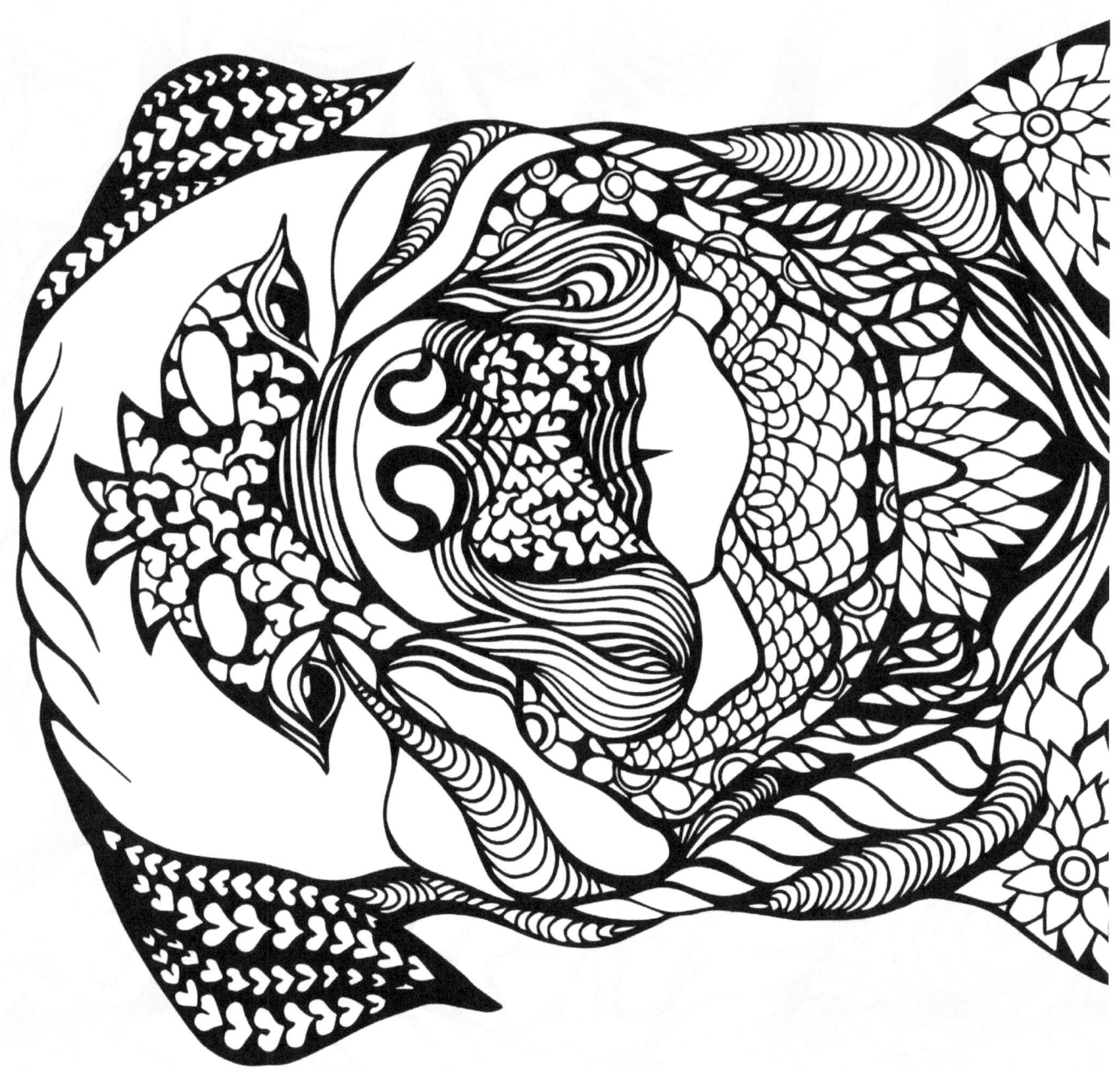

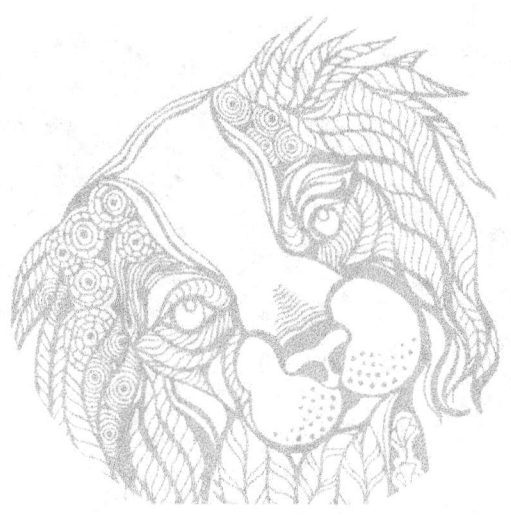

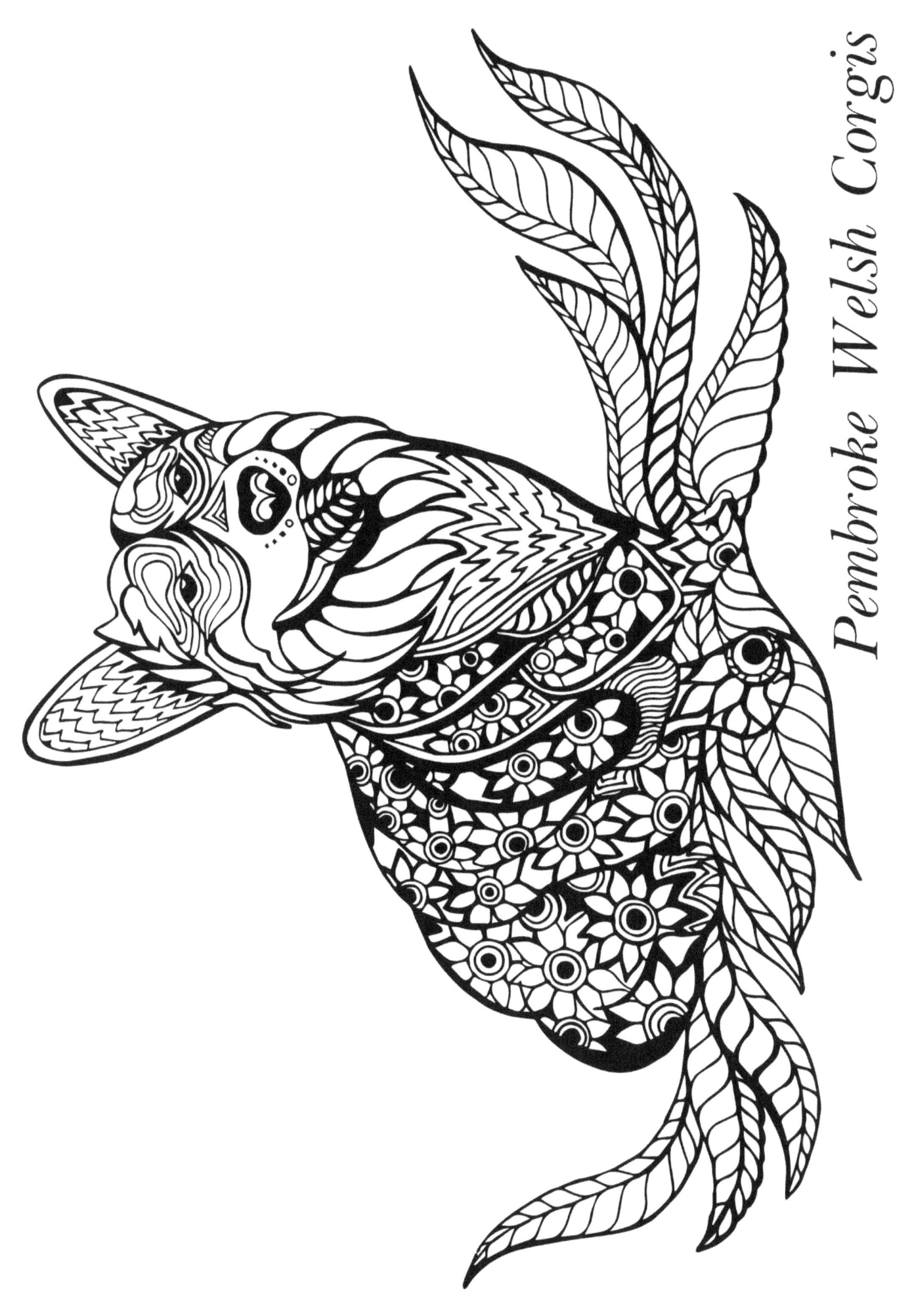

Pembroke Welsh Corgis

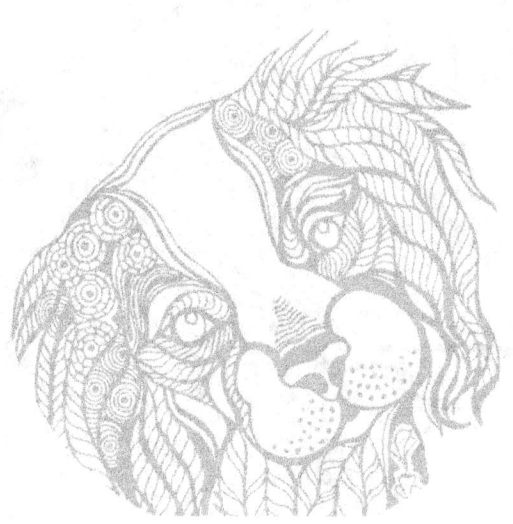

Mastiff

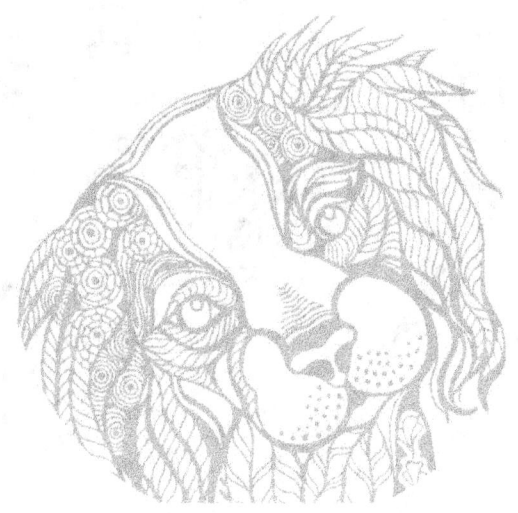

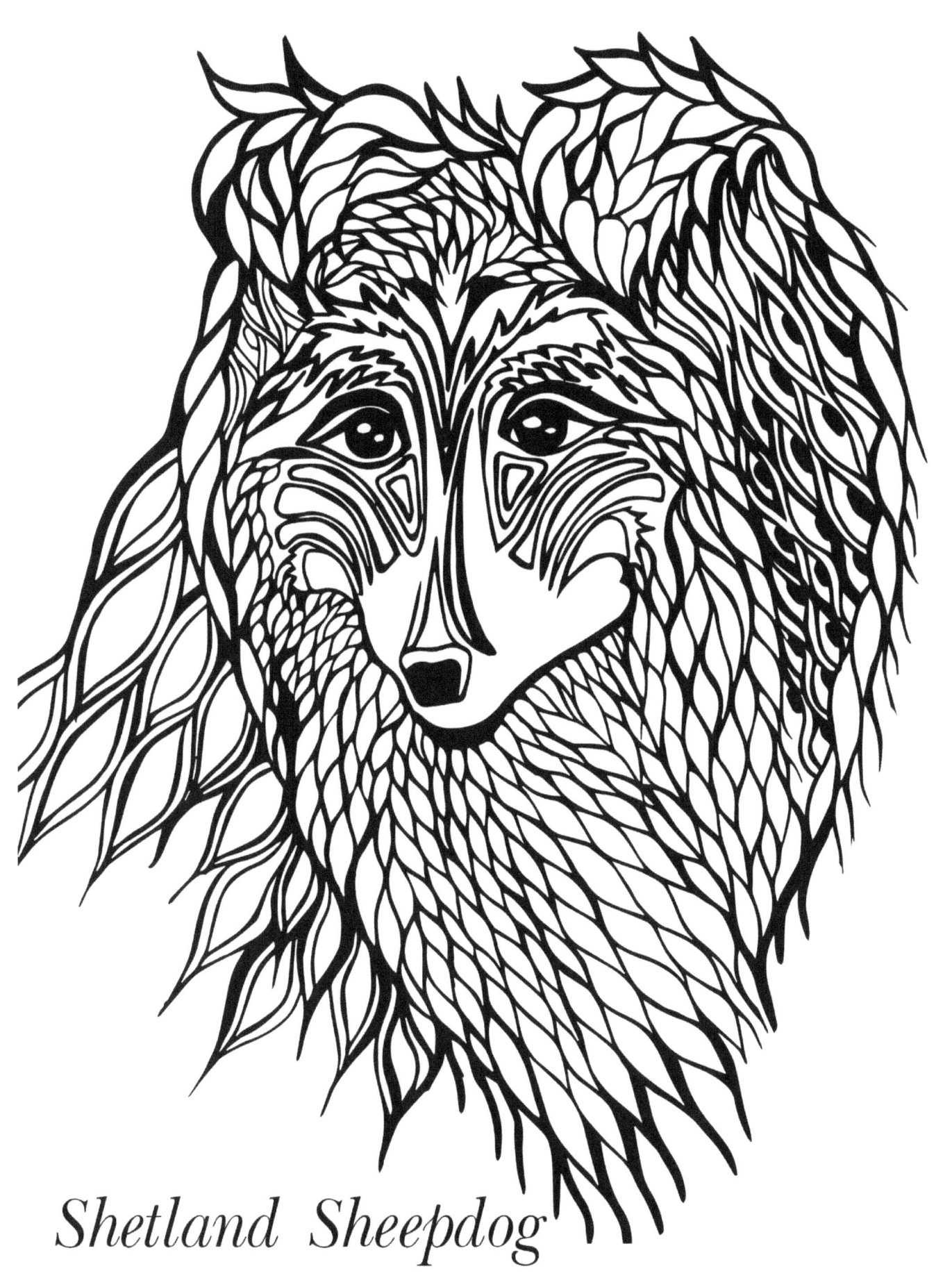

Shetland Sheepdog

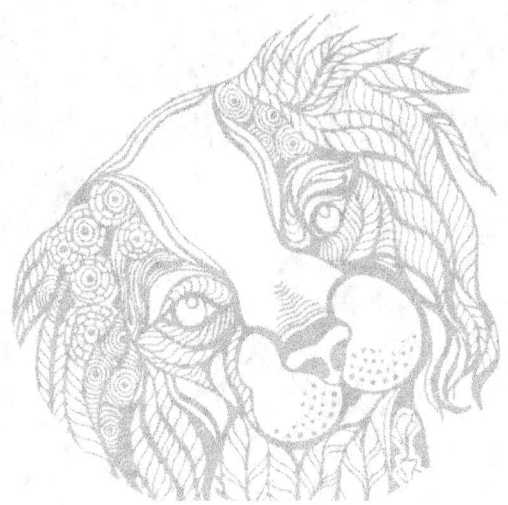

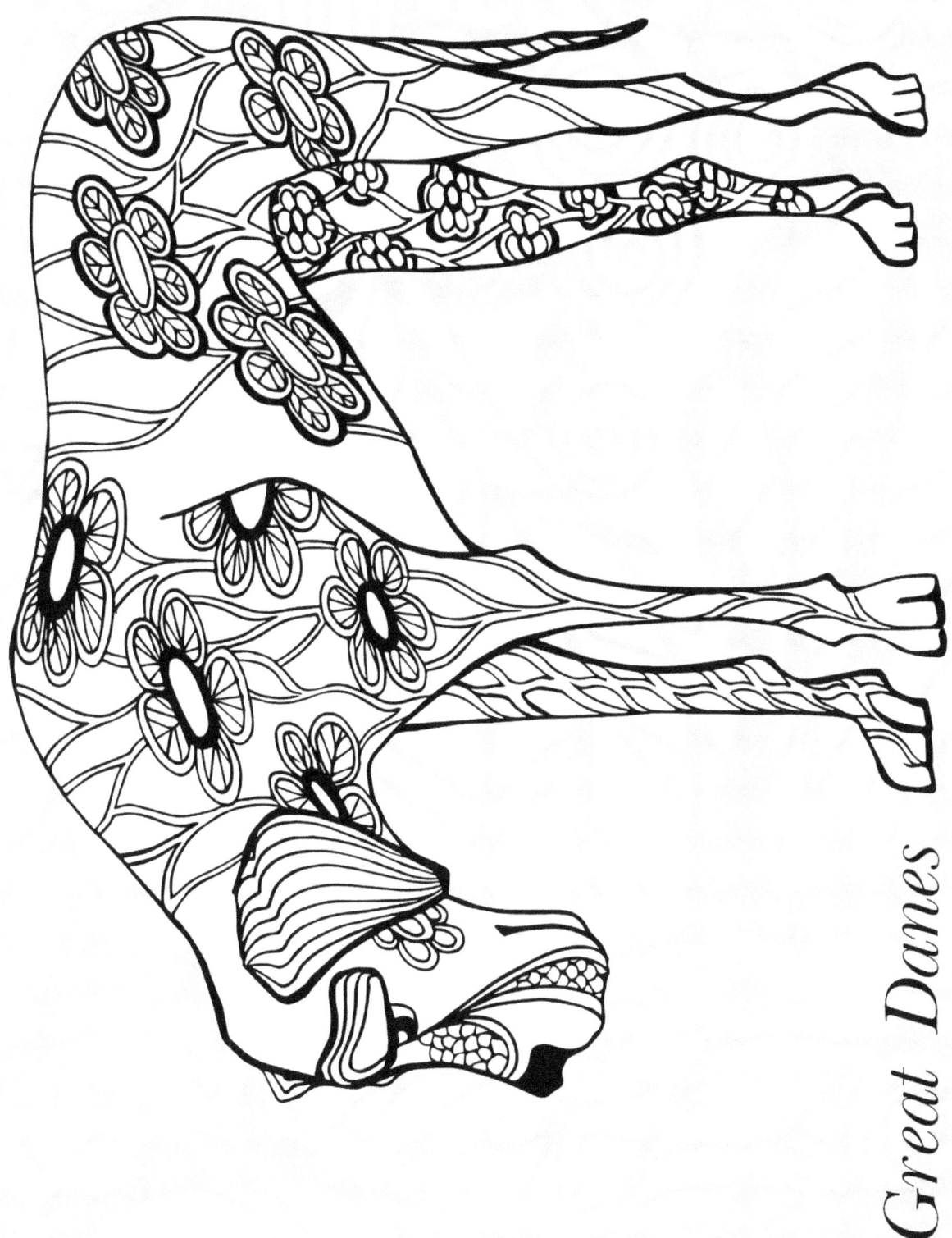

Great Danes

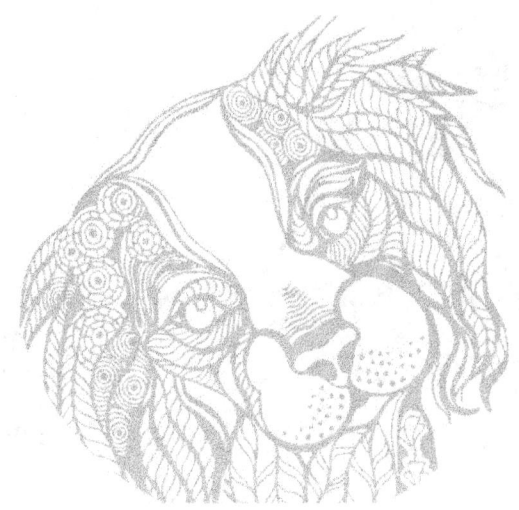

Havanese

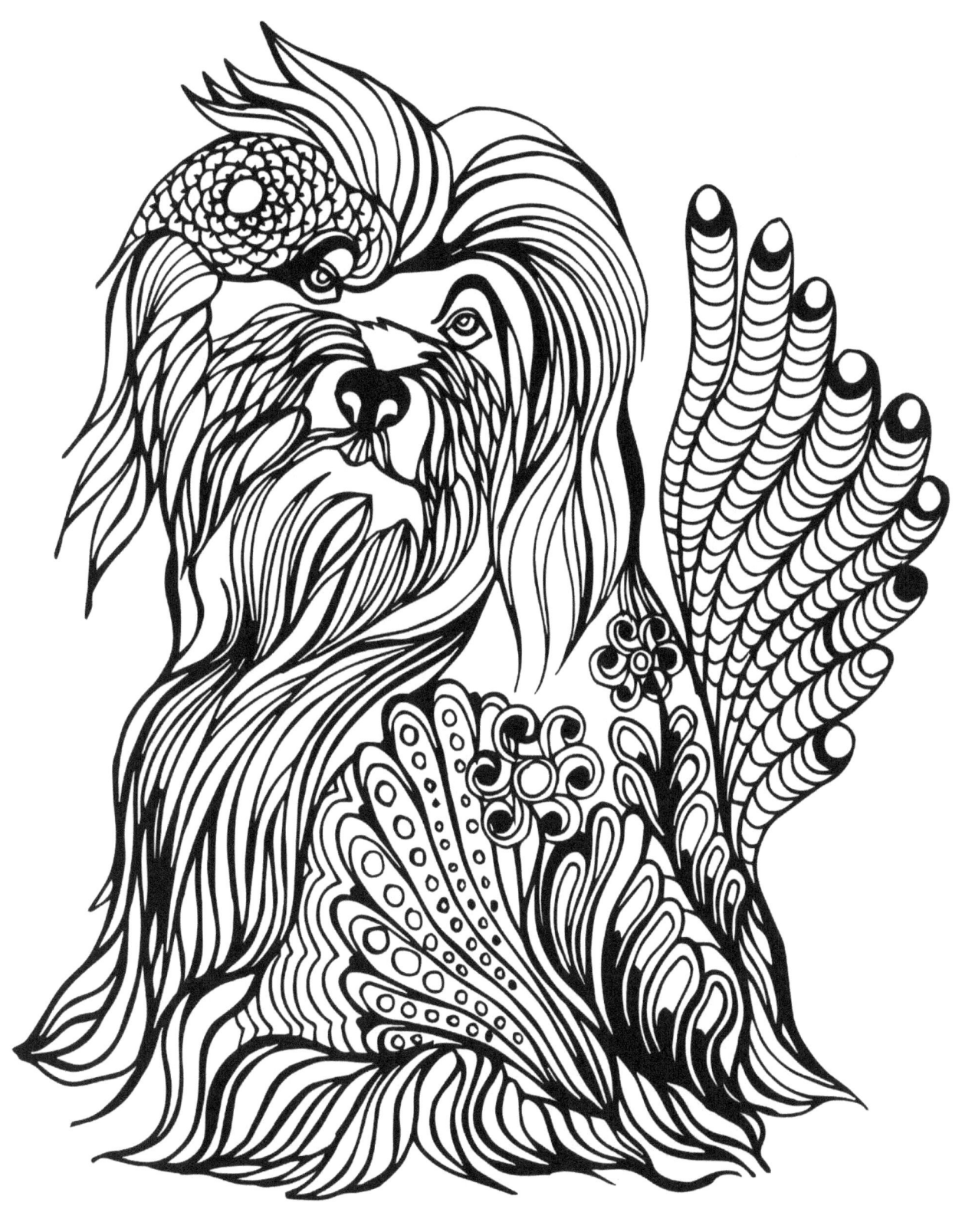

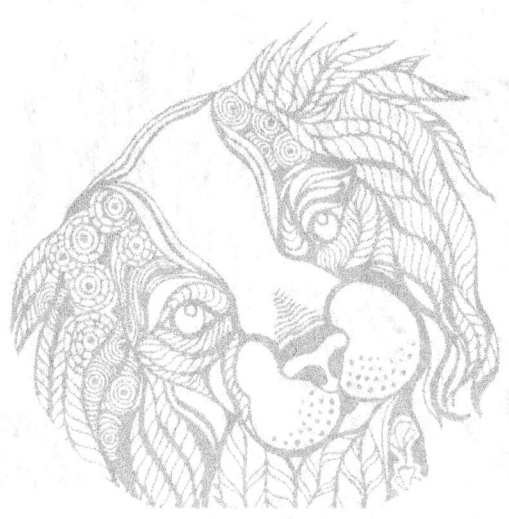

Brittanys

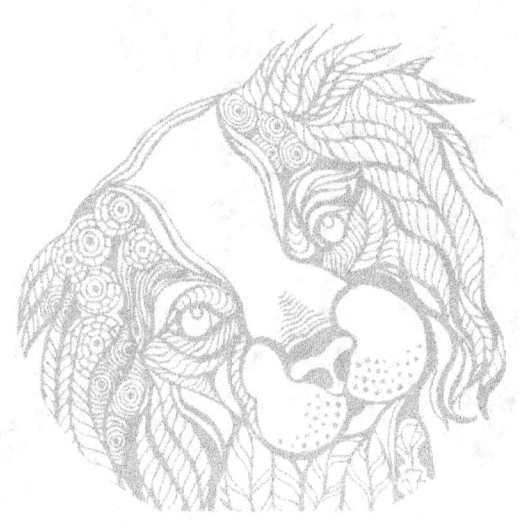

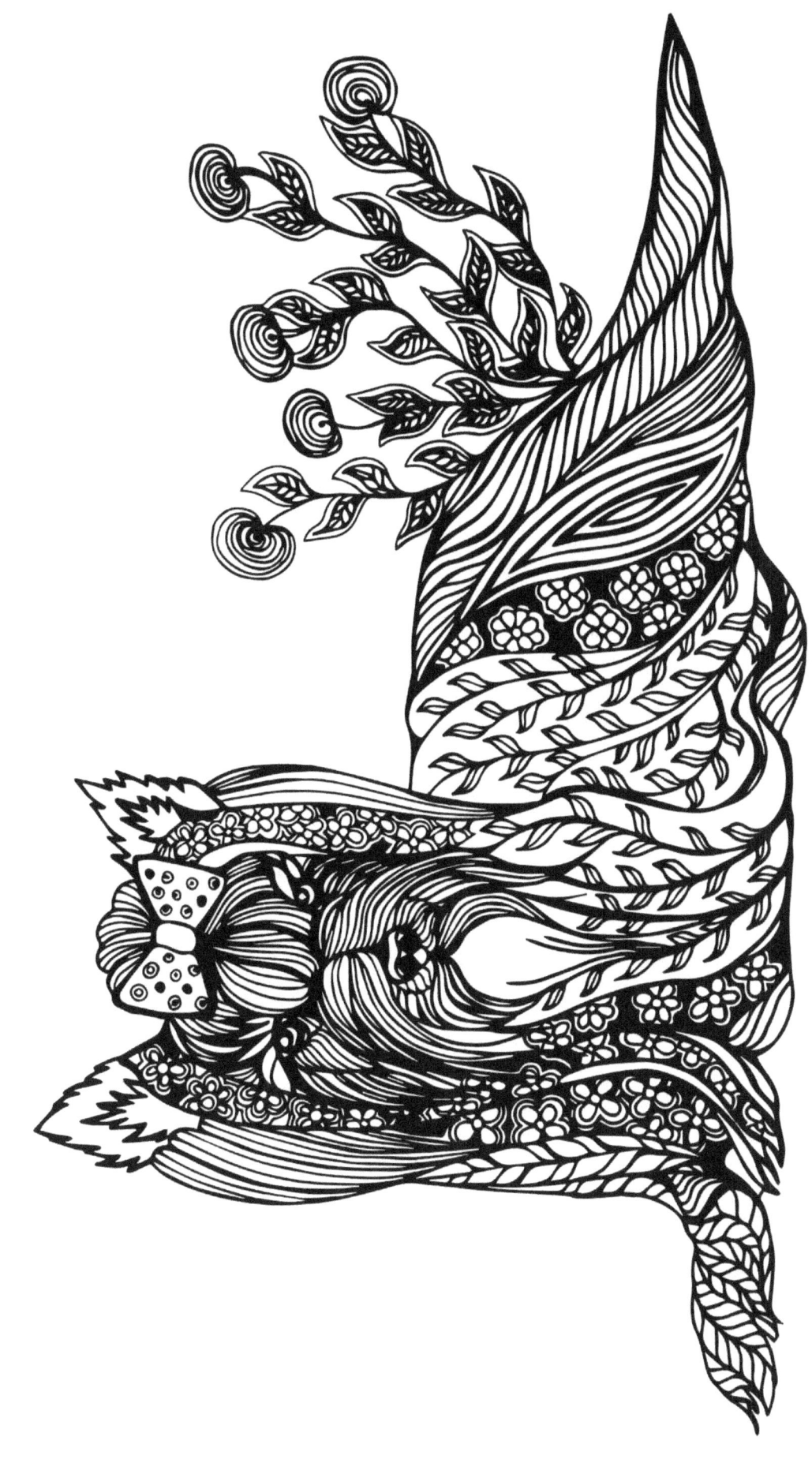

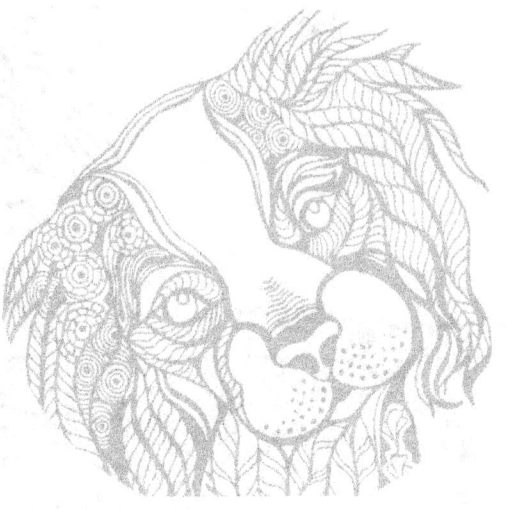

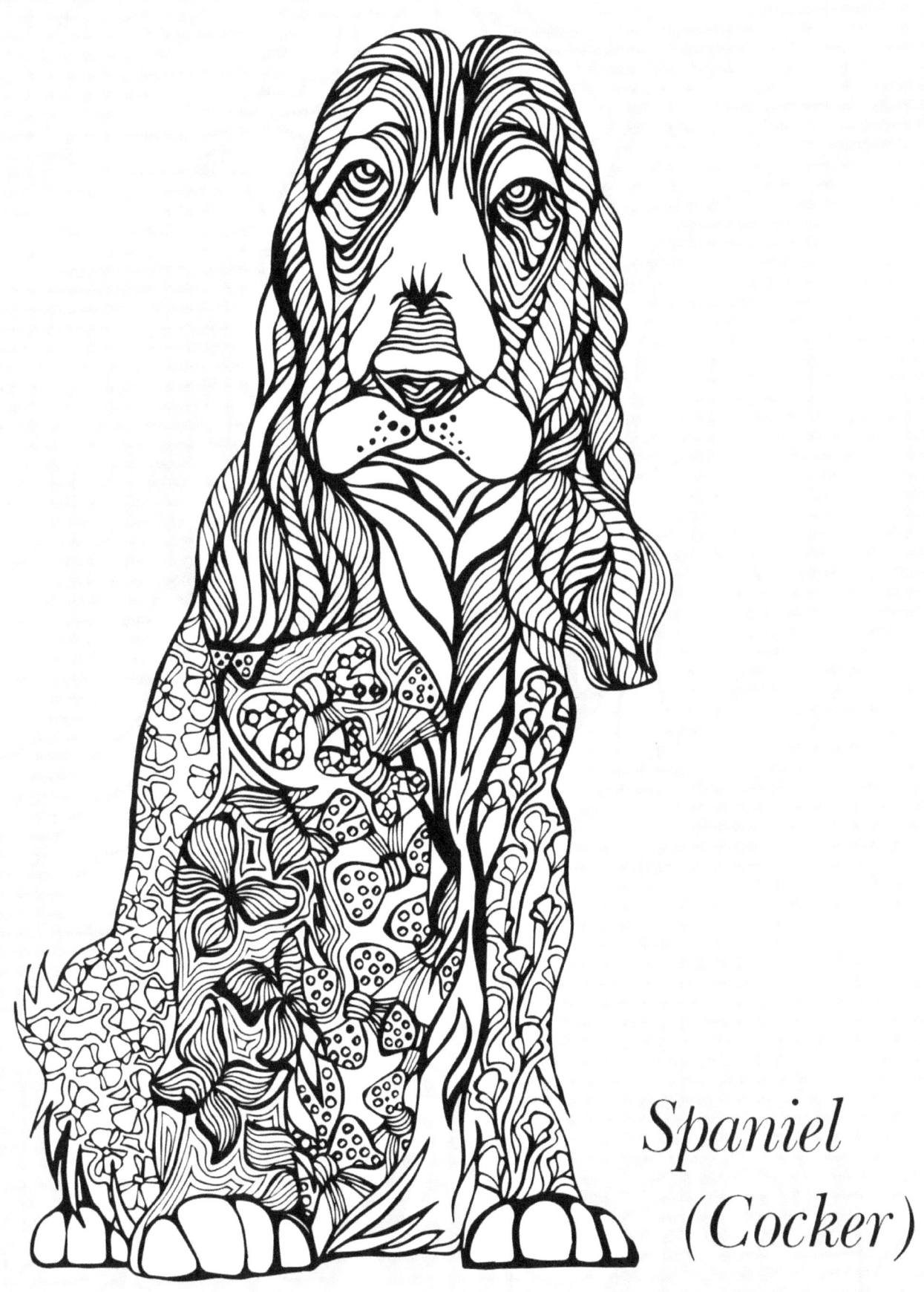

Spaniel
(Cocker)

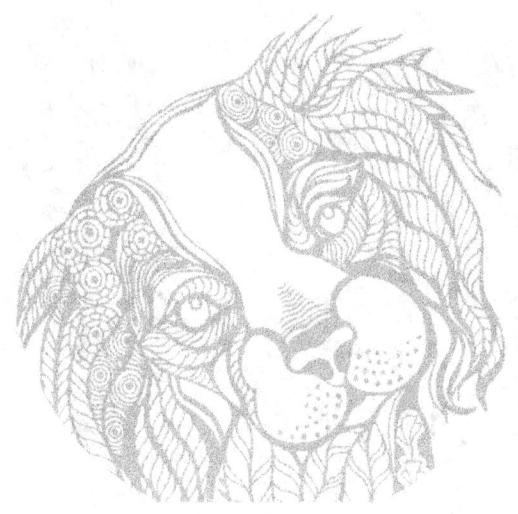

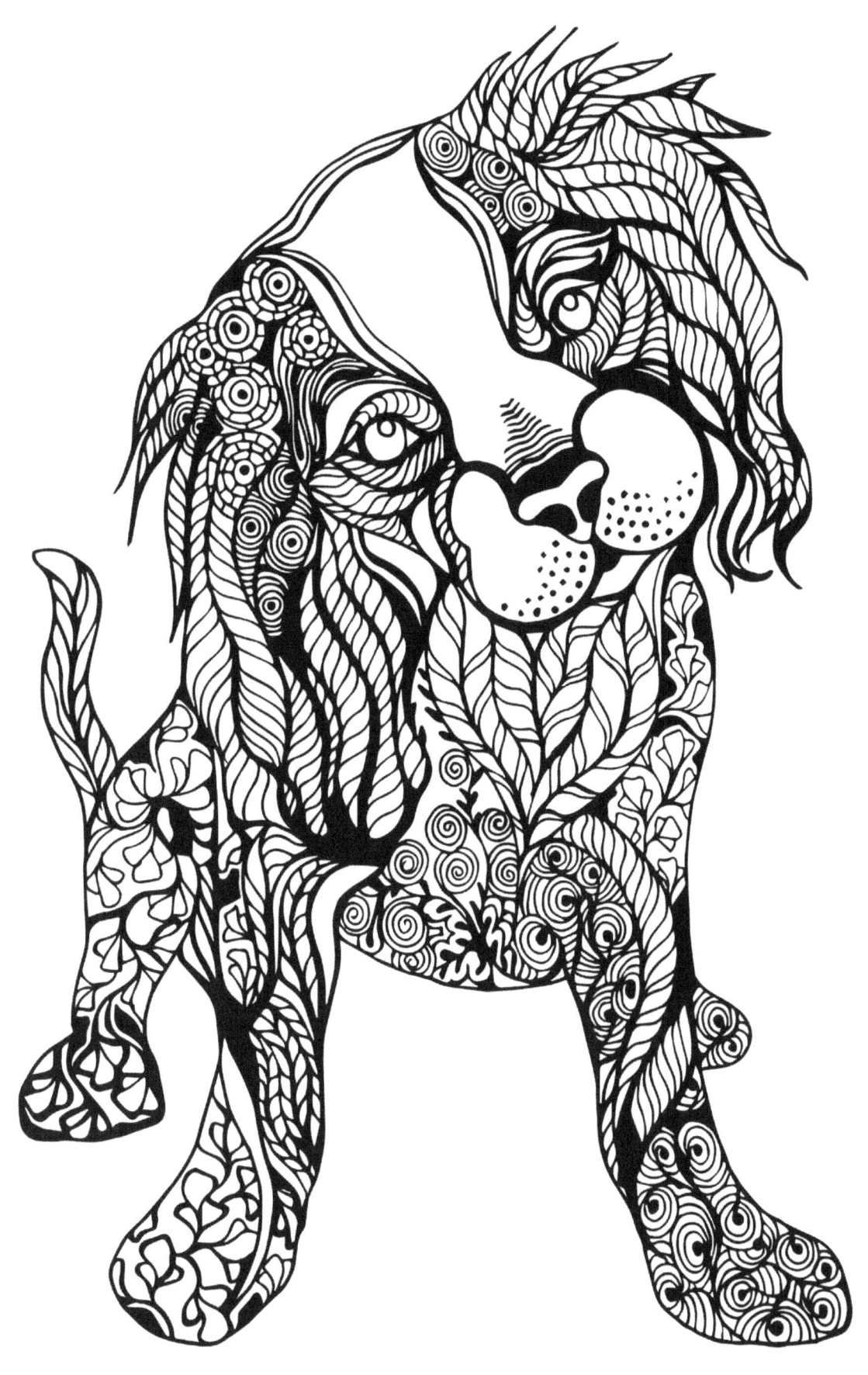

Cavalier King Charles Spaniel

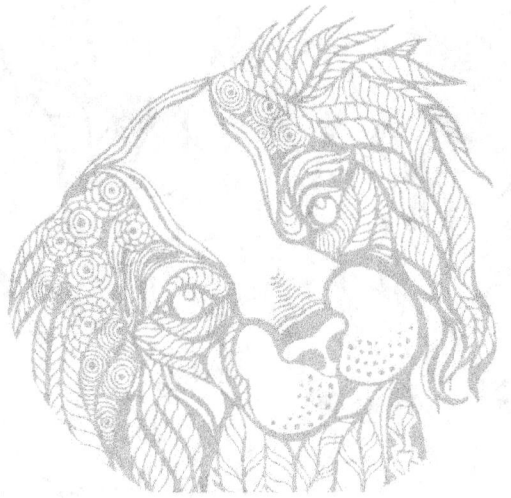

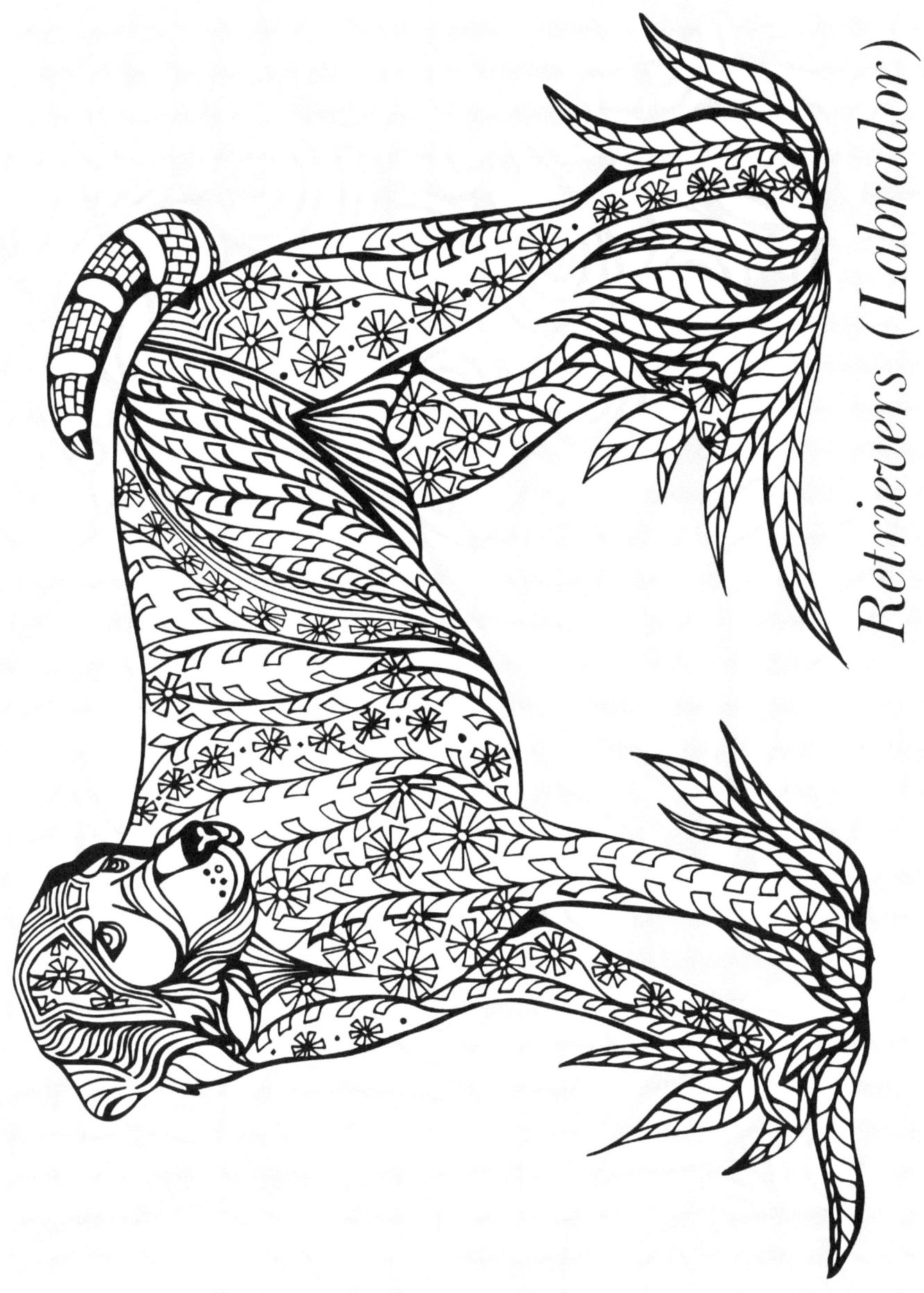

Retrievers (Labrador)

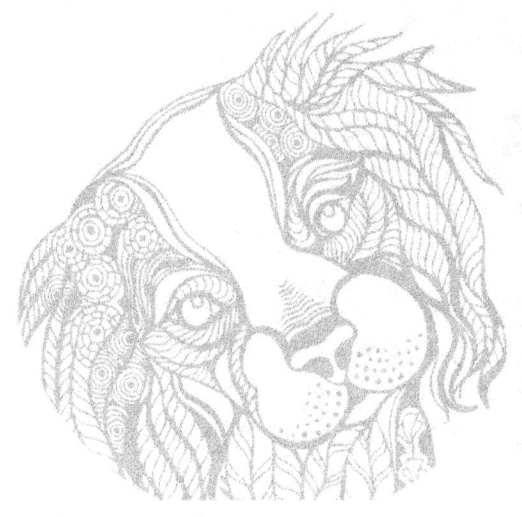

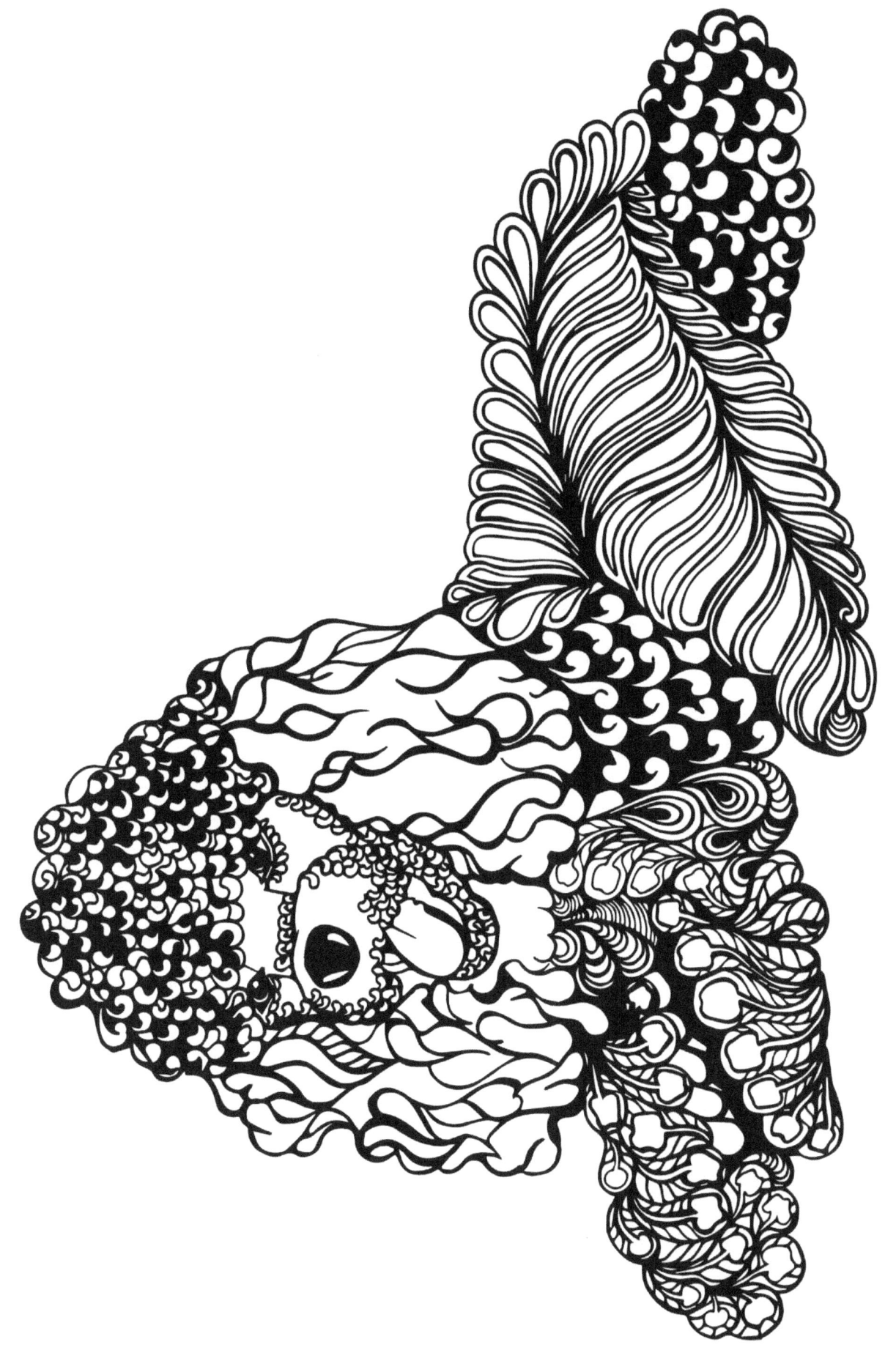

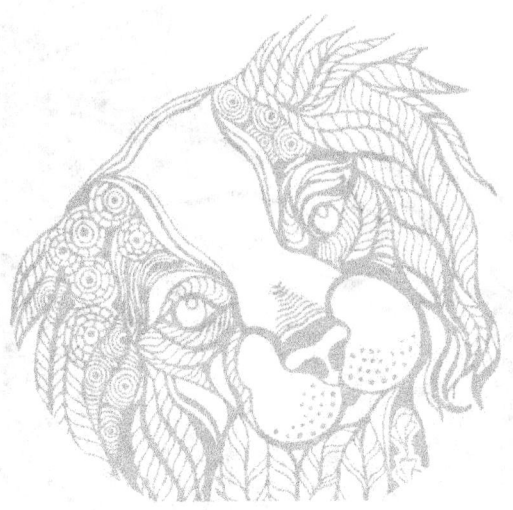

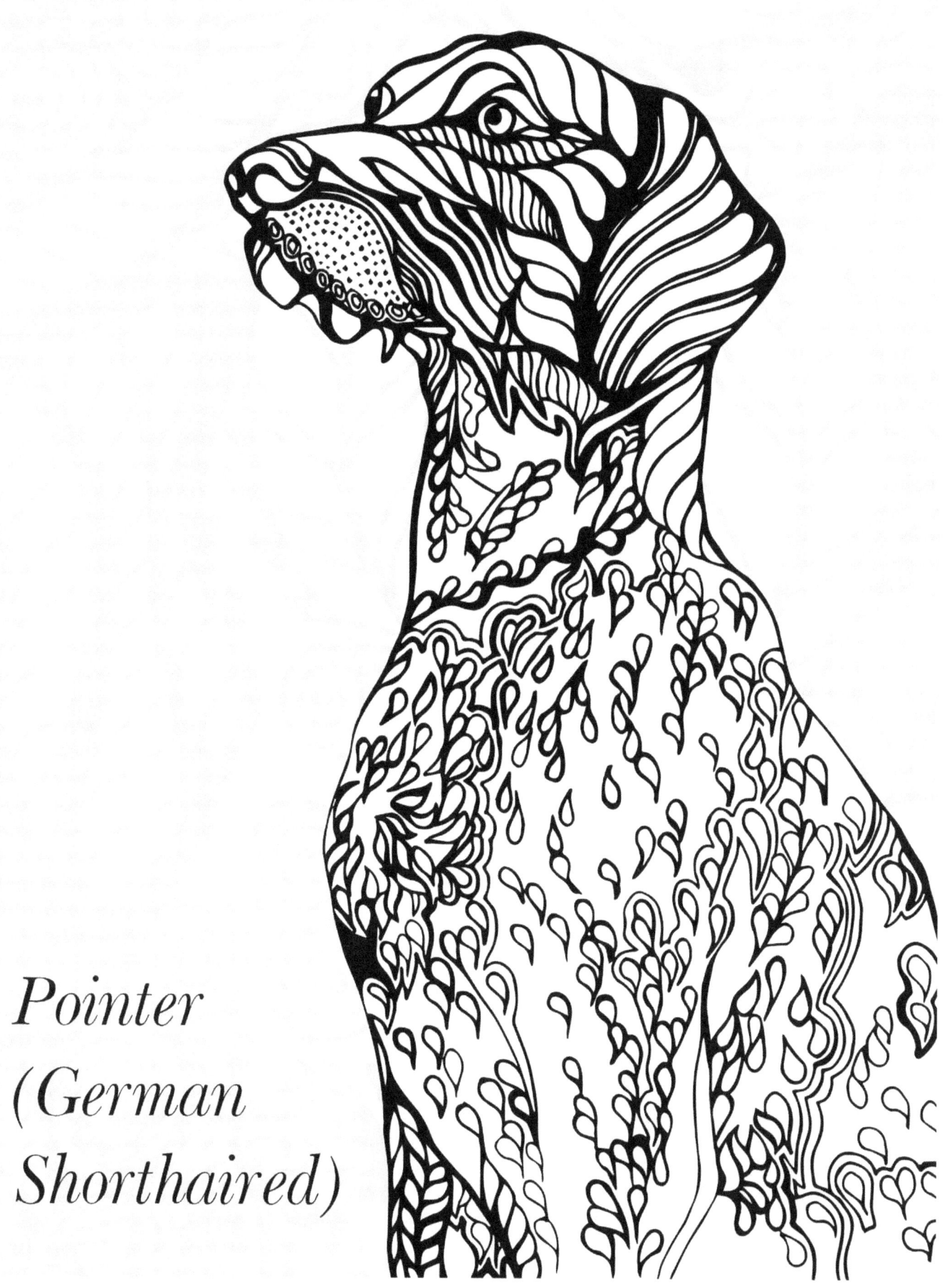

*Pointer
(German
Shorthaired)*

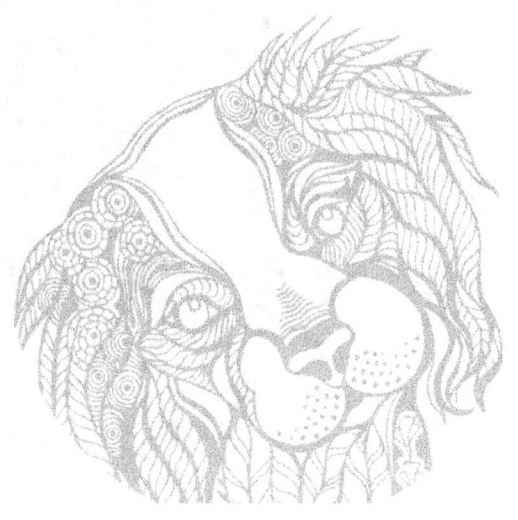

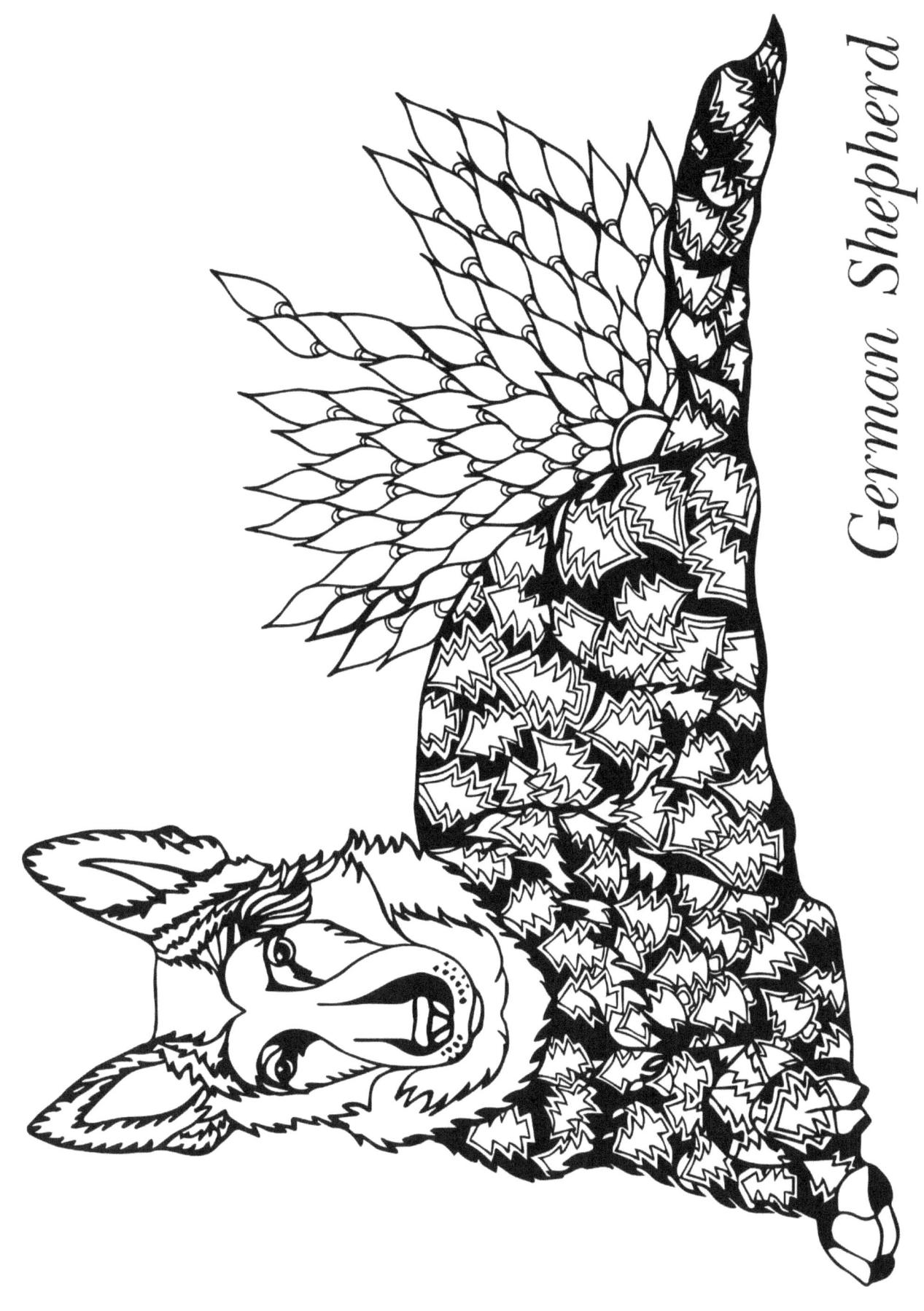

German Shepherd

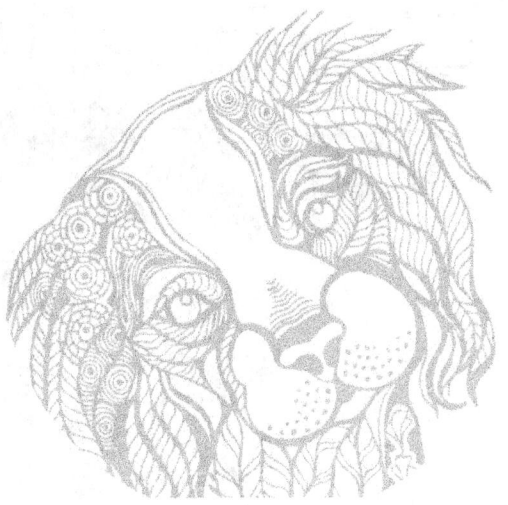

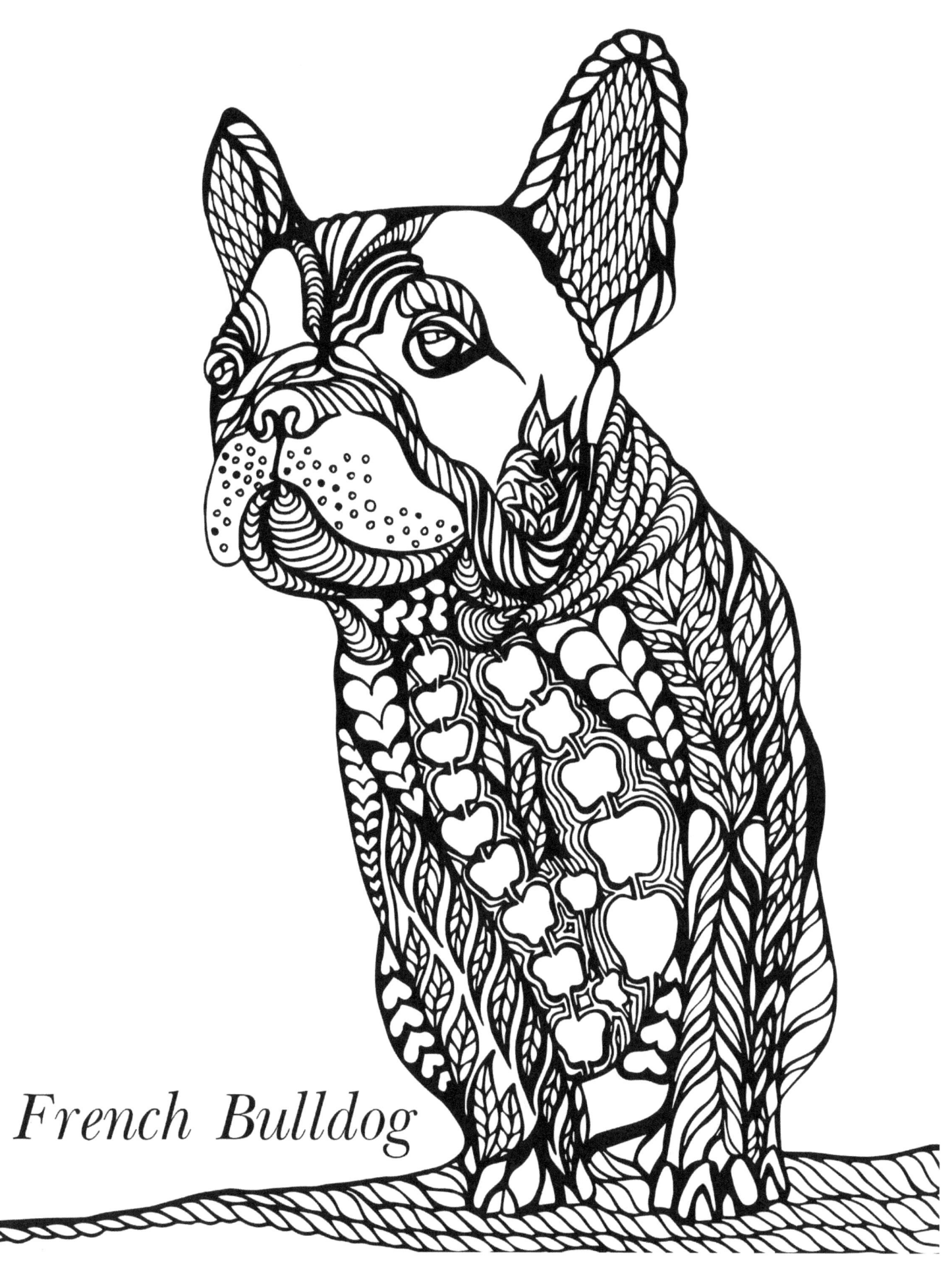

French Bulldog

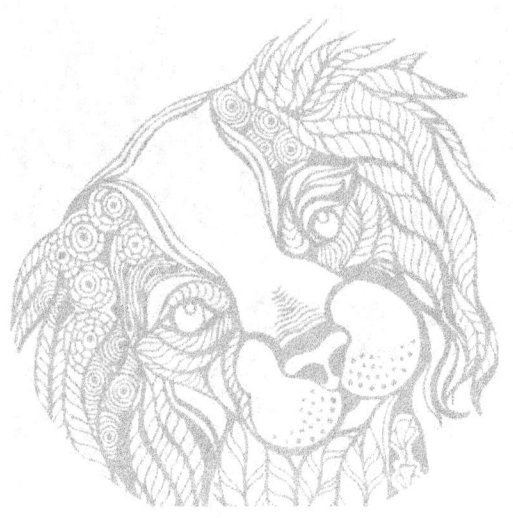

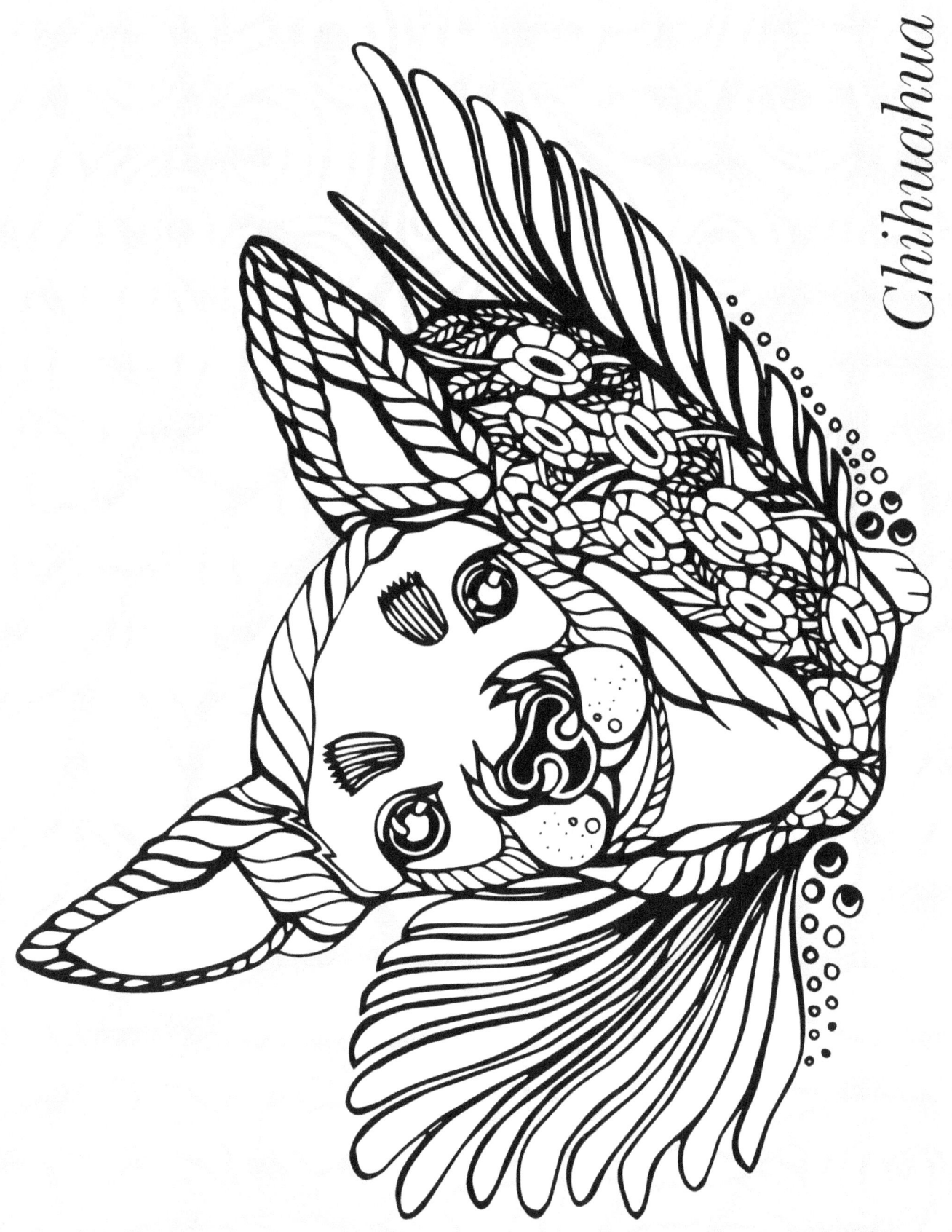

Chihuahua

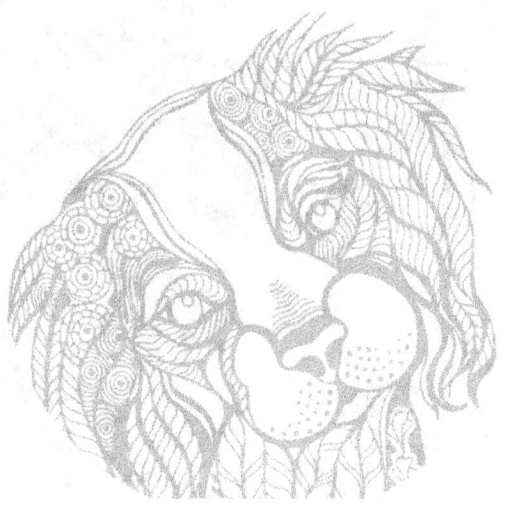

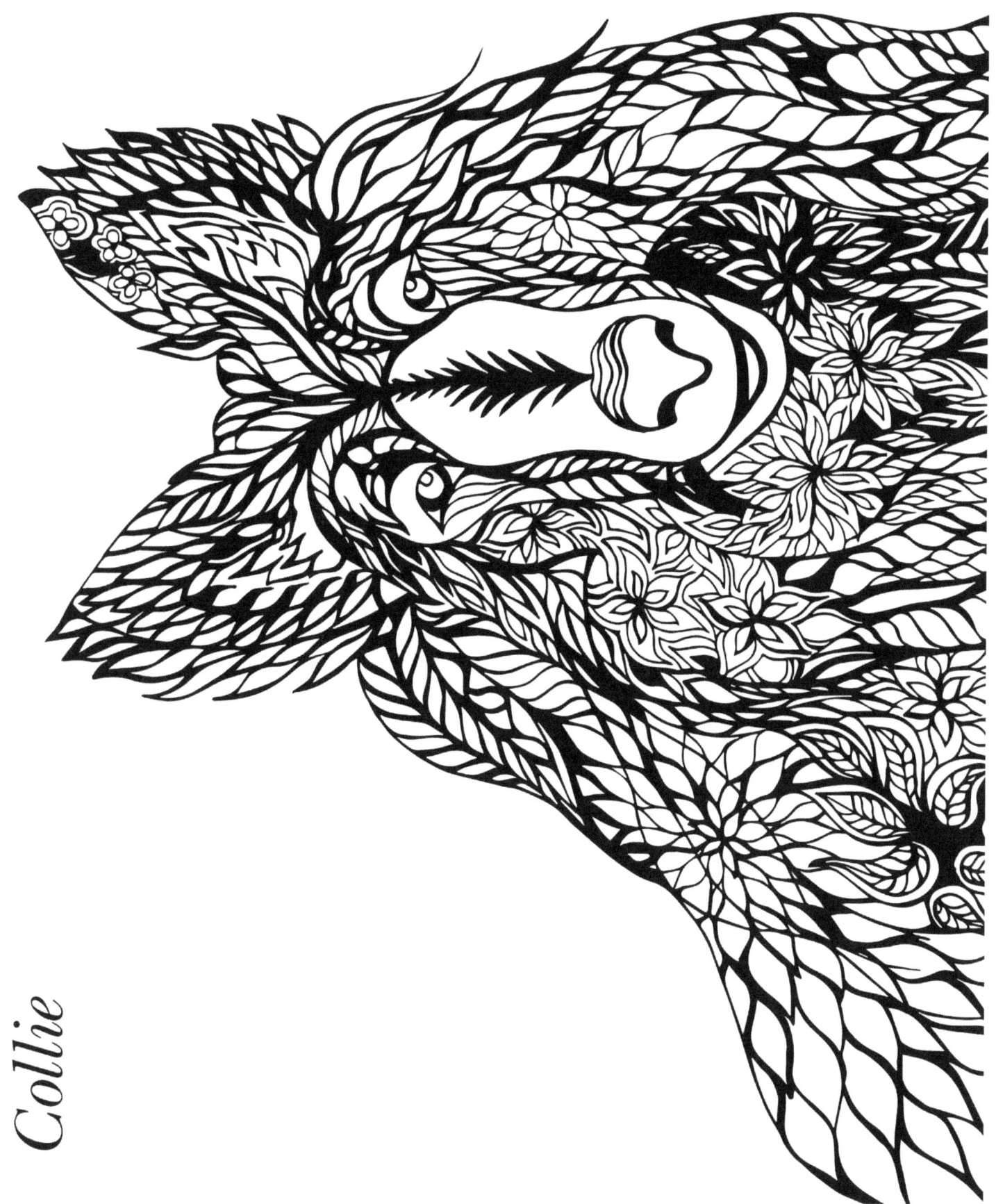

Collie

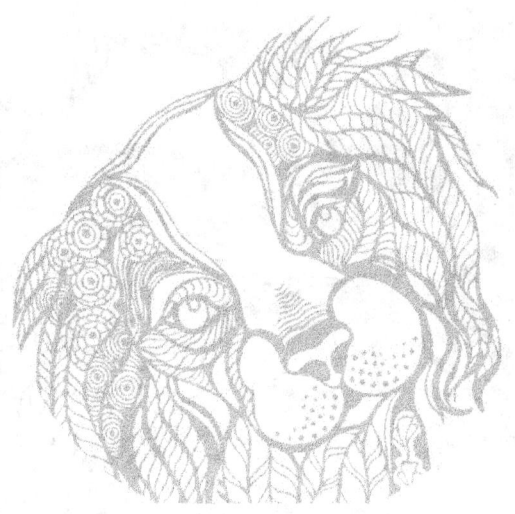

Maltese

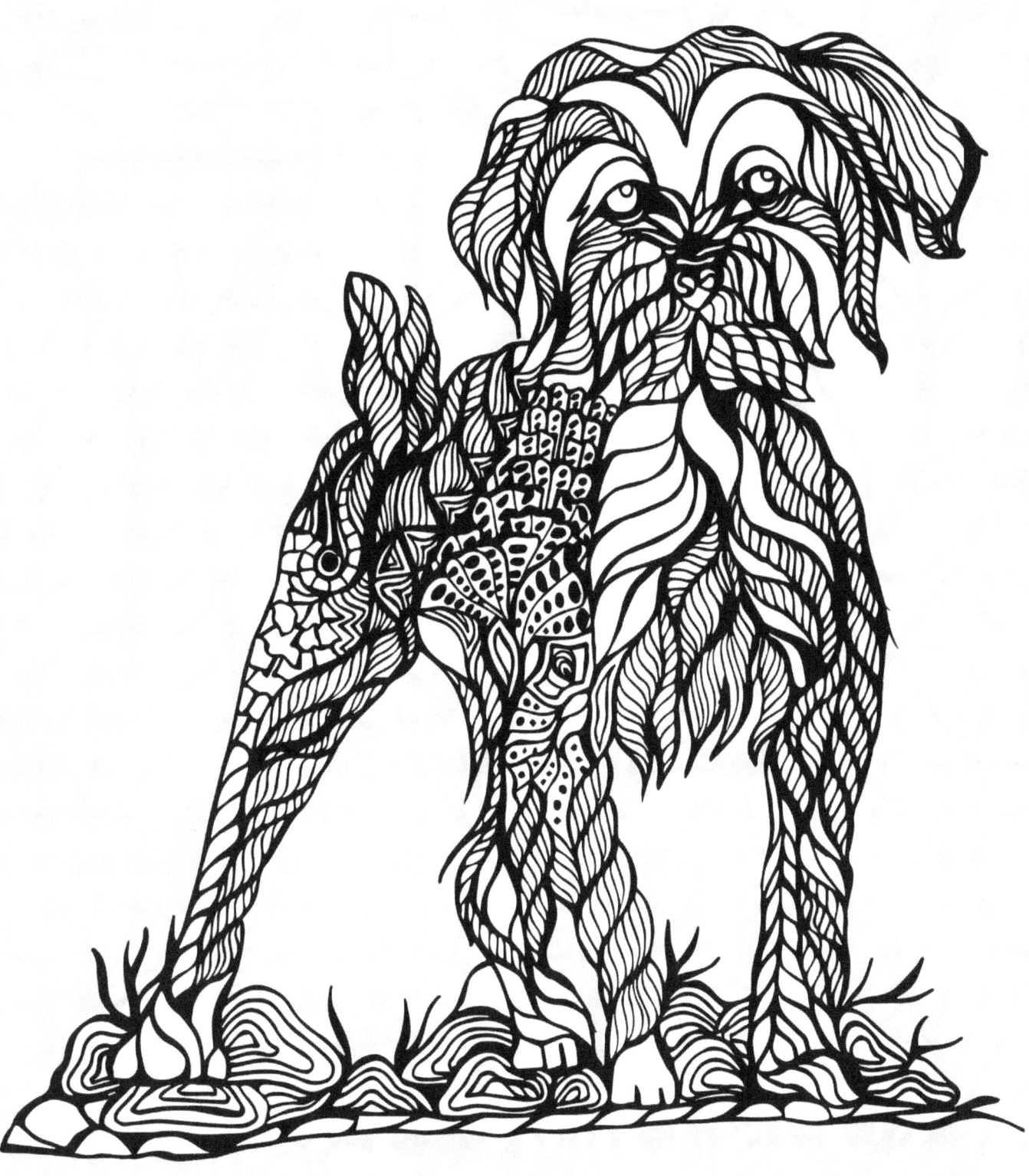

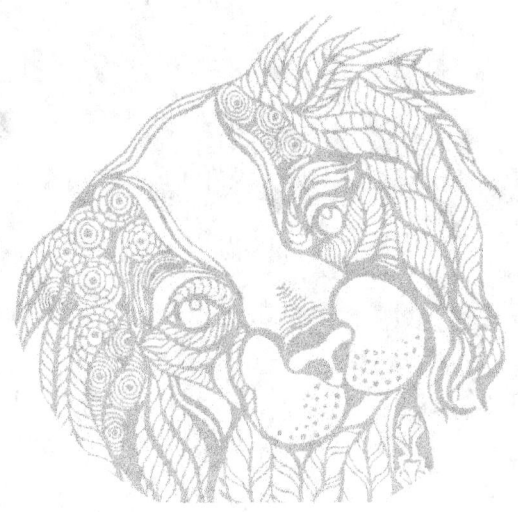

Pug

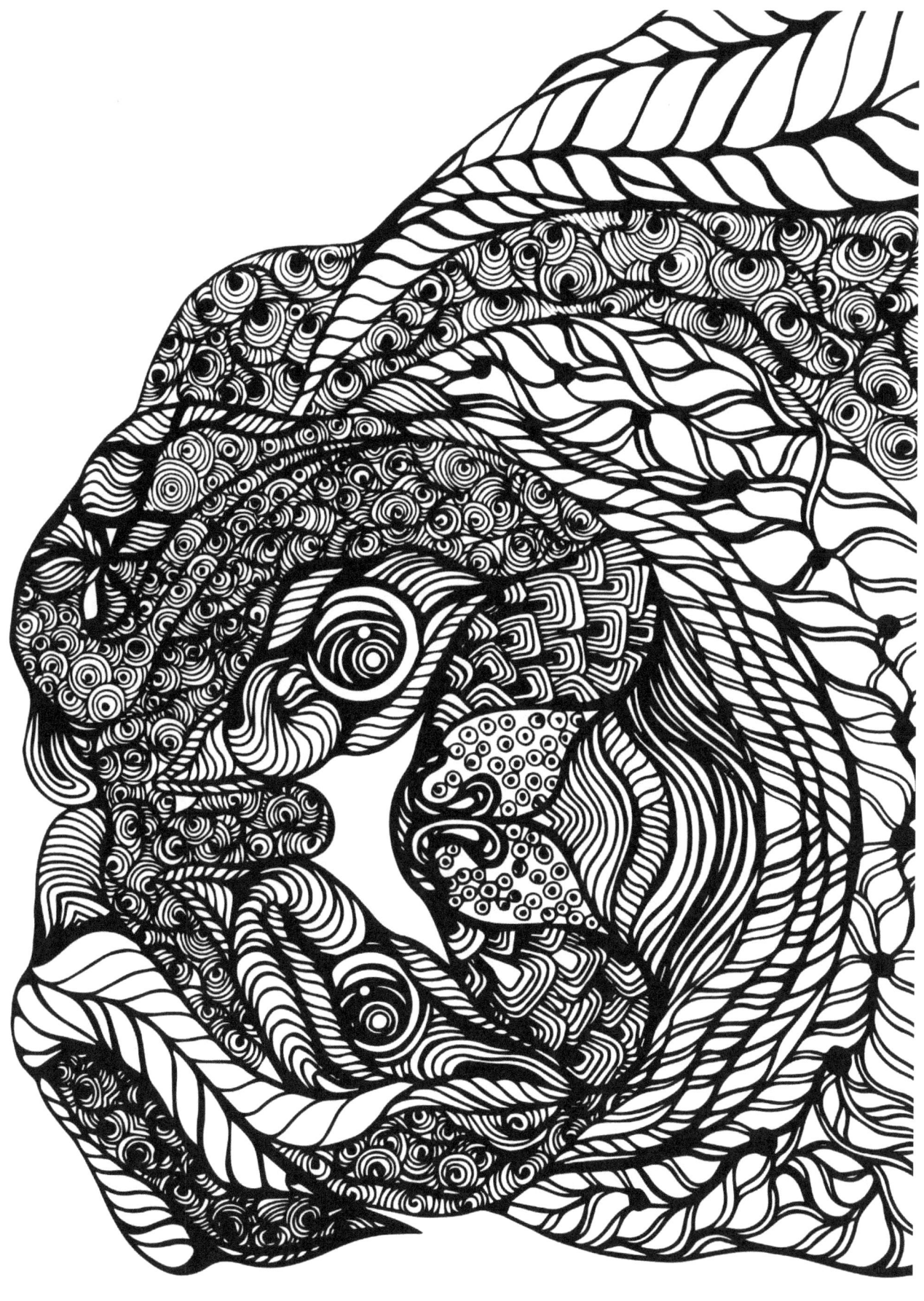

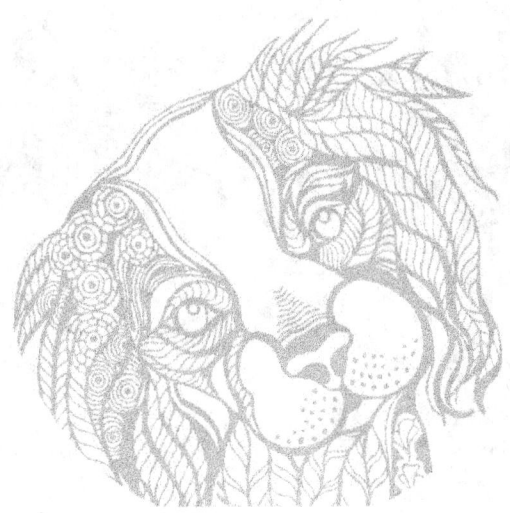

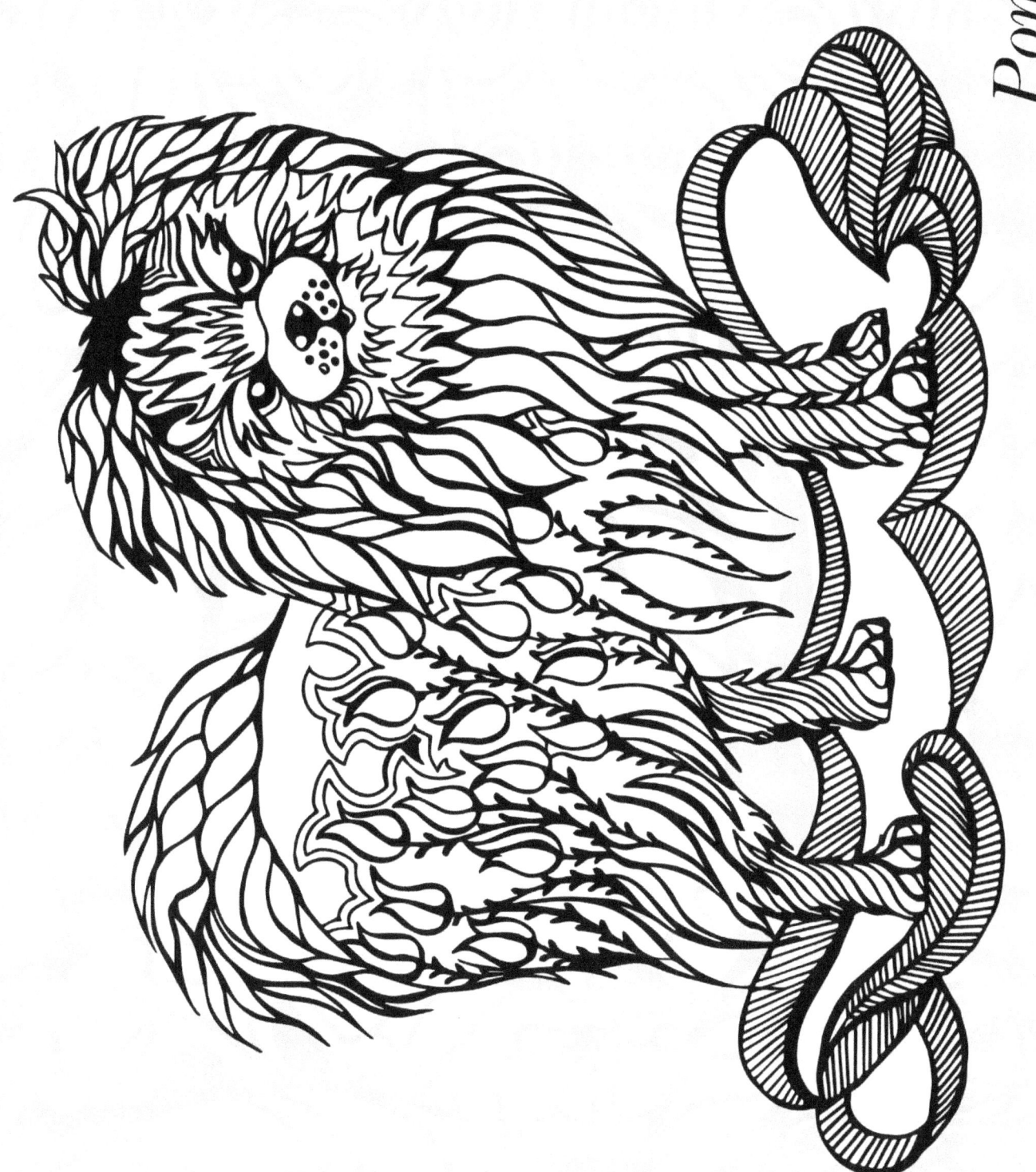

Pomeranian

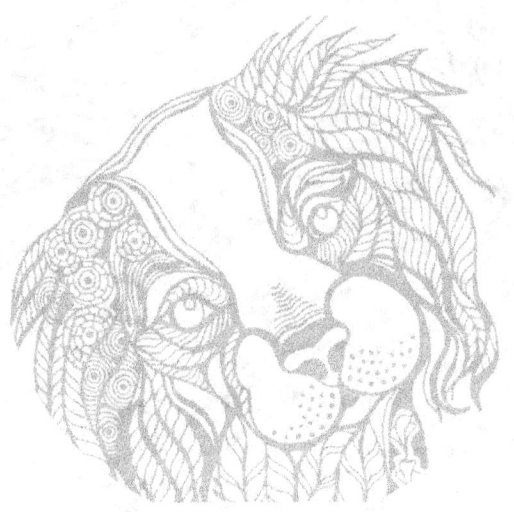

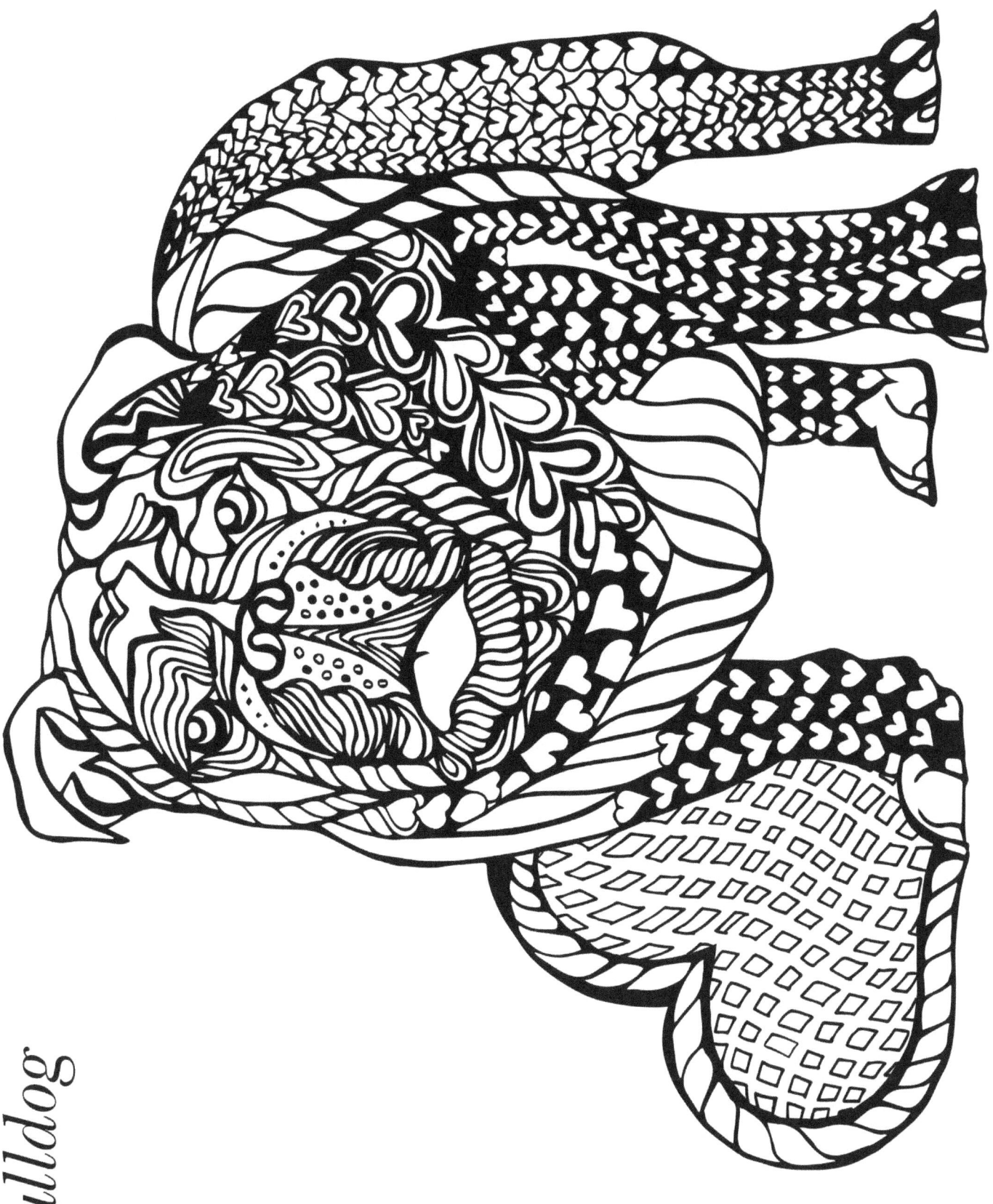

Bulldog

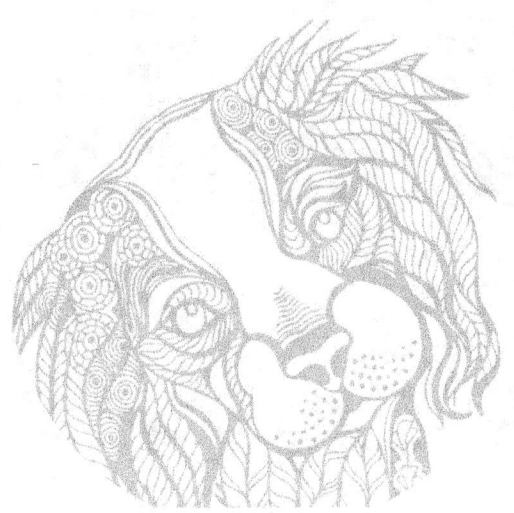

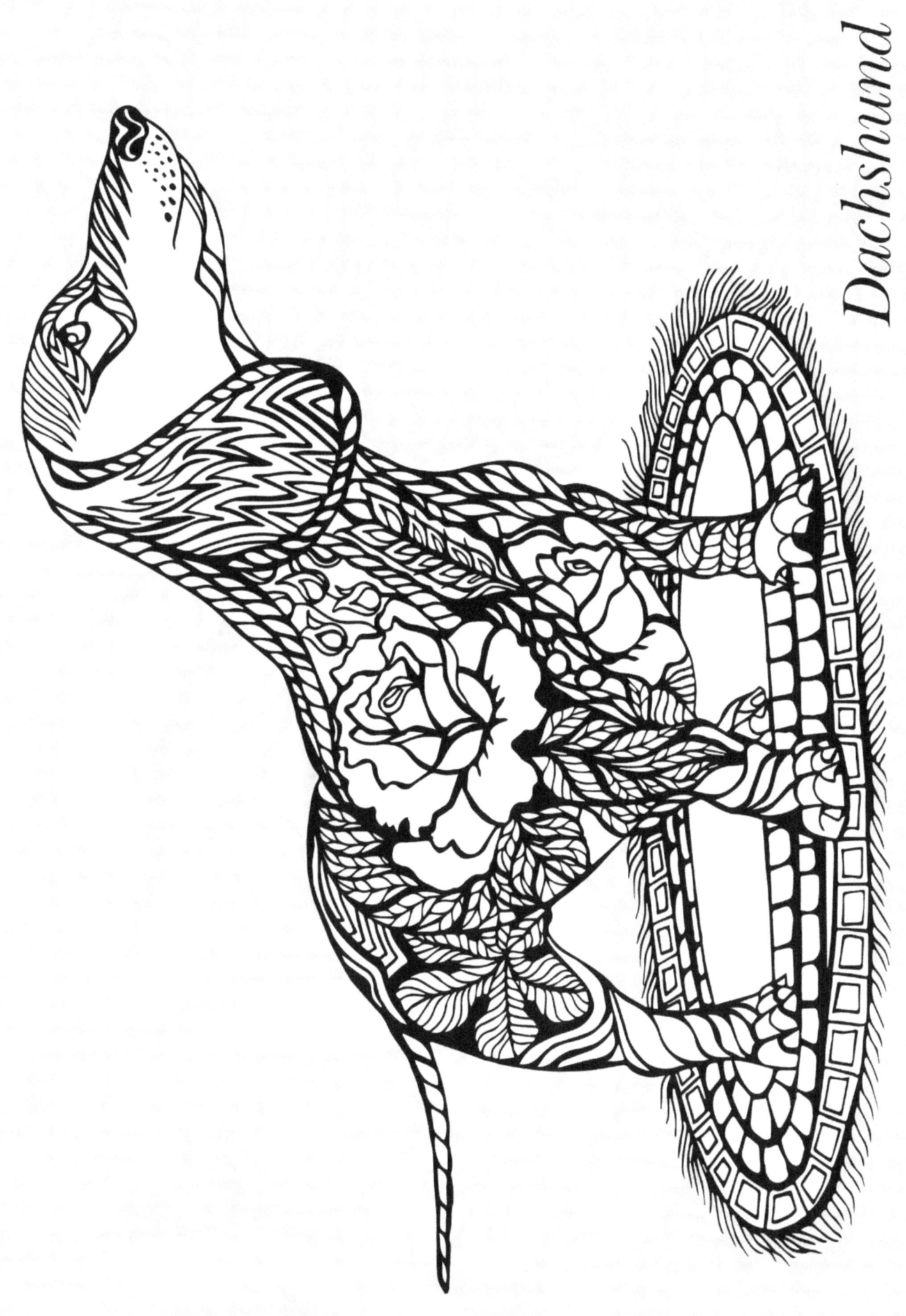

Dachshund

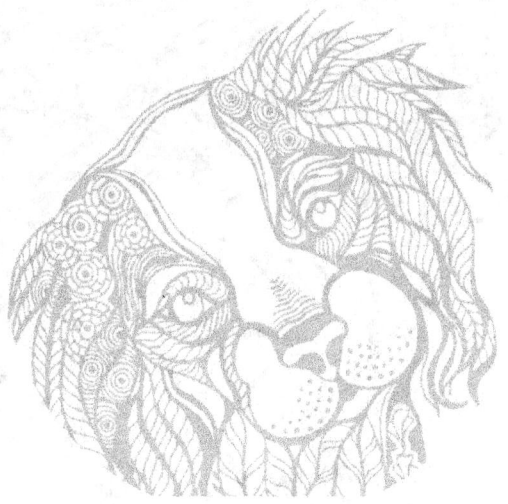

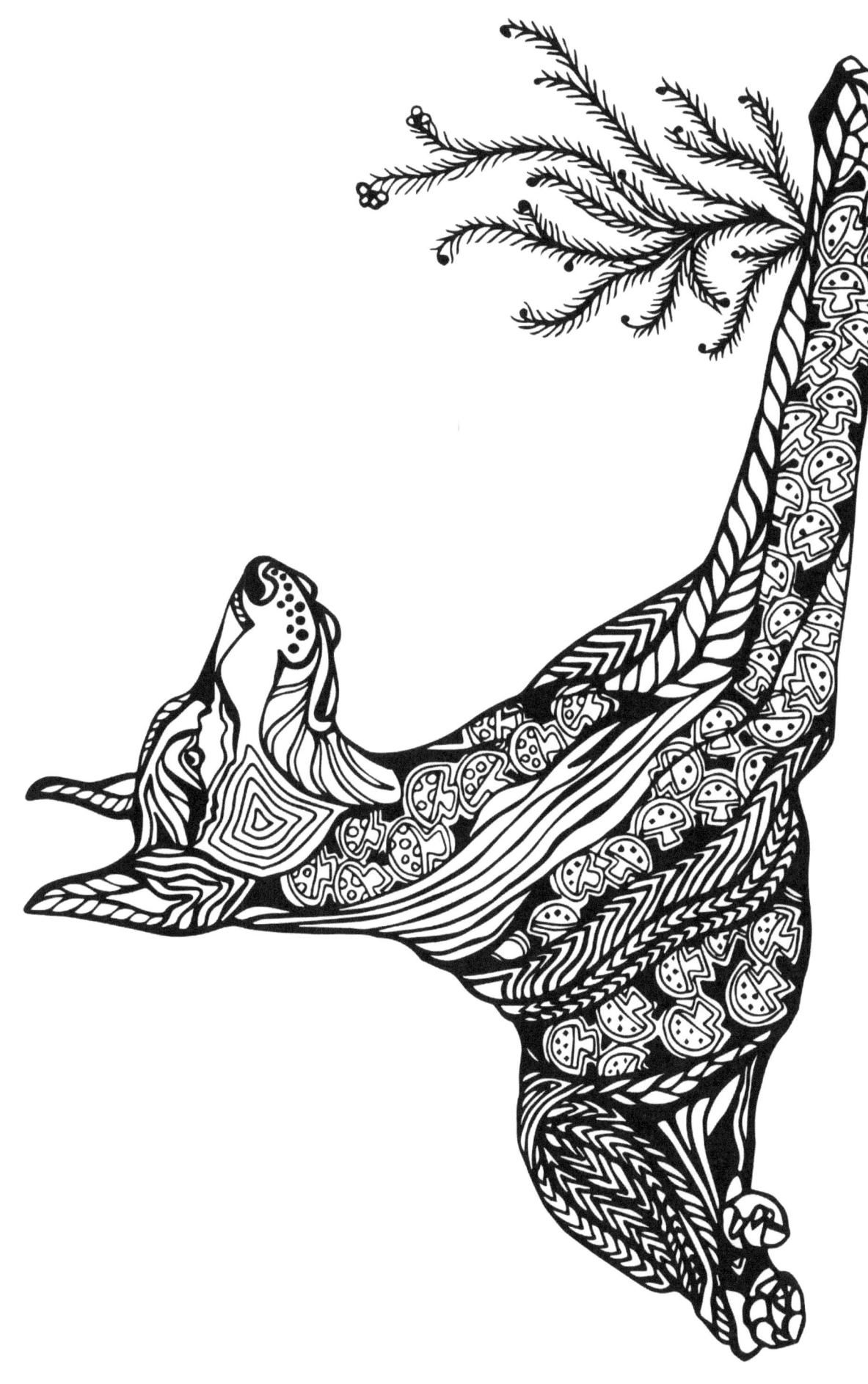

Doberman Pinscher

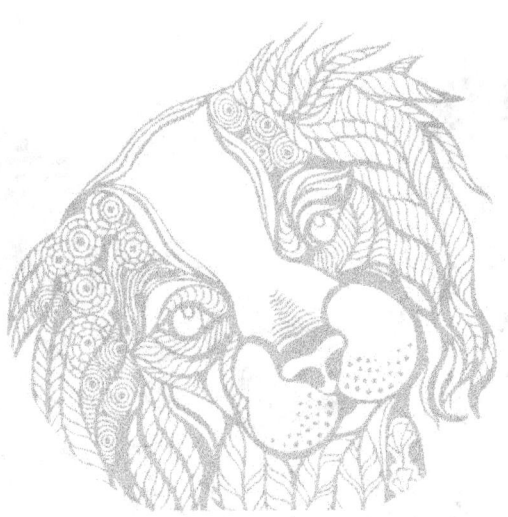

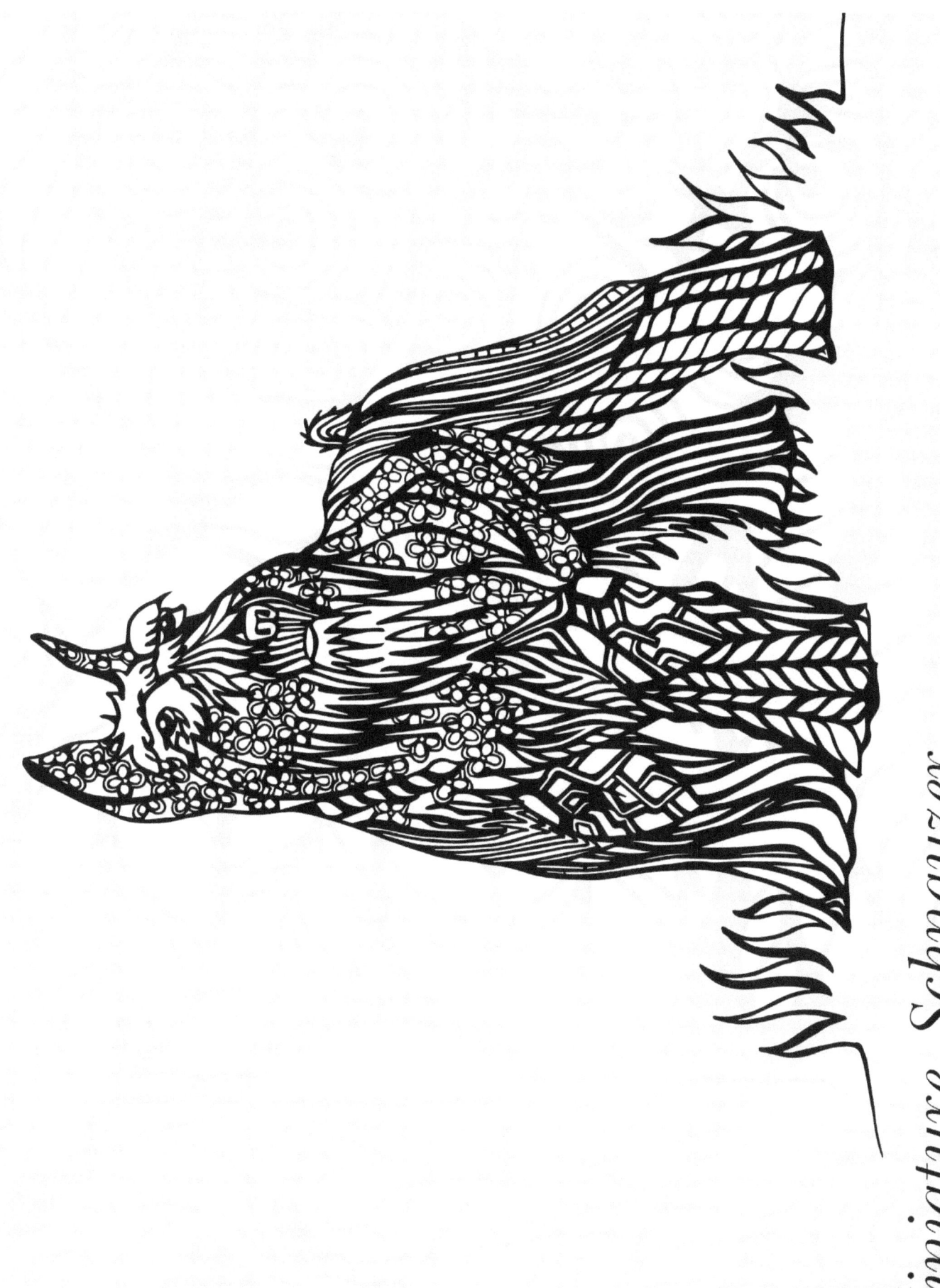

Miniature Schnauzer

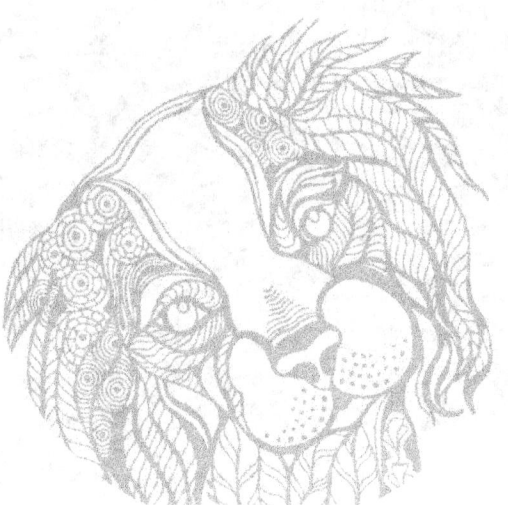

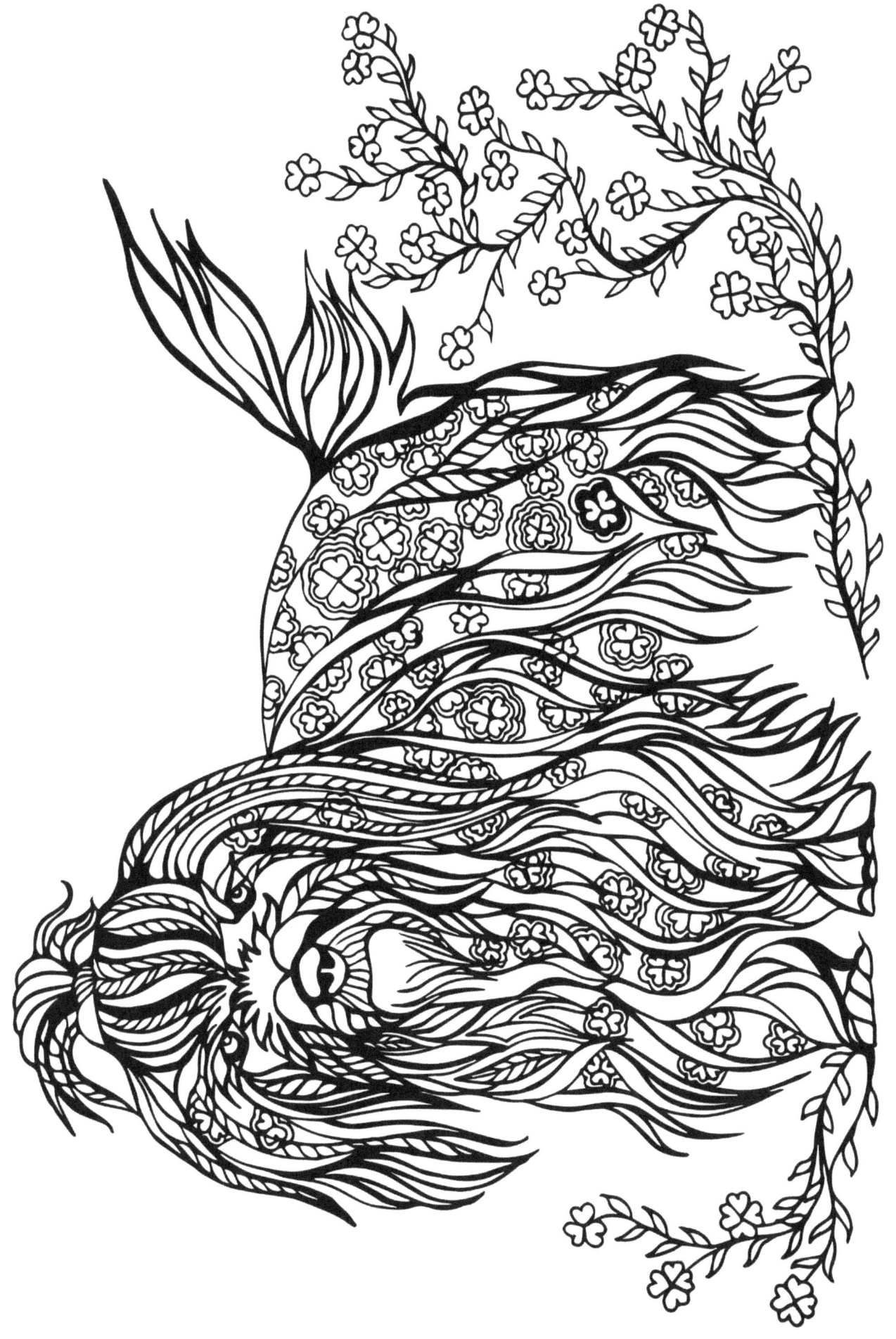

Shih Tzu

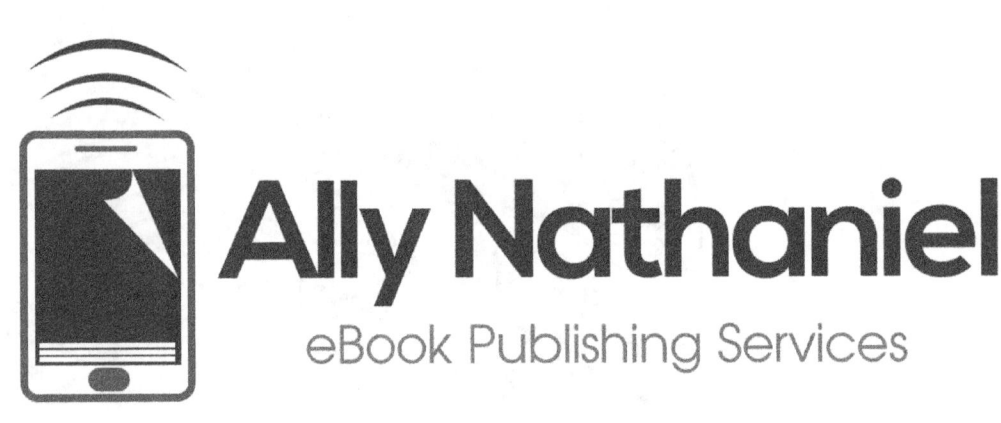

973-826-2020